# Damon Runyon

Twayne's United States Authors Series

Kenneth Eble, Editor
*University of Utah*

TUSAS 407

DAMON RUNYON
(1880–1946)
*Courtesy of the Director of the
Damon Runyon–Walter Winchell
Memorial Cancer Fund*

DISCARDED

# Damon Runyon

## By Patricia Ward D'Itri

*Michigan State University*

*Twayne Publishers • Boston*

*Damon Runyon*

Patricia Ward D'Itri

Copyright © 1982 by G. K. Hall & Company
Published by Twayne Publishers
A Division of G. K. Hall & Company
70 Lincoln Street
Boston, Massachusetts 02111

Book production by Marne B. Sultz
Book design by Barbara Anderson

Printed on permanent/durable acid-free
paper and bound in The United States of
America.

**Library of Congress Cataloging in Publication Data**

D'Itri, Patricia Ward.
Damon Runyon.

(Twayne's United States authors series; TUSAS 407)
Bibliography: pp. 160-164
Includes index.
1. Runyon, Damon, 1880–1946–Criticism and
interpretation. I. Title. II. Series.
PS3535.U52Z63          818′.5409          81-7095
ISBN  0-8057-7336-3                    AACR2

# Contents

# About the Author

Patricia Ward D'Itri was born in Saginaw, Michigan. Her doctoral dissertation explored Samuel Taylor Coleridge's theories of literary criticism. At Michigan State University she has taught English as a Second Language and Major Currents in American Social and Literary Thought. She is presently a professor of American Thought and Language and teaches Women in America. Her interest in Damon Runyon was renewed as part of the academic study of popular culture that has emerged in recent years. She had originally been attracted to Runyon's humor in popular magazines and anthologies.

Like popular culture, the roles of minorities and women have increasingly been included as part of D'Itri's research on literary and social currents in American life. This was reflected in papers delivered on the Black American novelist Richard Wright, Michigan history, and the role of women. D'Itri is also the coauthor of several papers and one book on mercury contamination of the environment.

# Preface

Two words, "Runyonese" and "Runyonesque," were coined as Damon Runyon's short fiction became something of a fad in the United States and Great Britain in the 1930s. Best known for his distinctive "slanguage" and grammatical structure oriented around the present tense, Runyon's short stories about Broadway hoodlums attracted steadily larger numbers of readers when they appeared in such national magazines as *Cosmopolitan, Collier's,* and the *Saturday Evening Post.* Collected editions of the short stories and serialization in the *London Evening Standard* newspaper increased the furor among British readers who either imitated or rejected Runyon's language.

A successful New York newspaper reporter and columnist, Runyon was widely respected for articles on sports, crime, and humorous anecdotes about the human condition before his first Broadway story was published in 1929. His status as a newspaperman overshadowed that of author for some years after his death in 1946. The musical comedy *Guys and Dolls,* however, and movie adaptations of the short stories, have kept before the general public Runyon's Broadway tales of hoods and racetrack touts who frequented Mindy's Restaurant as well as various speakeasies. The boisterous humor with which Runyon chronicled their activities attracted readers and movie patrons especially during Prohibition when breaking the law was something of a national pastime. Runyon satirized the activities of the gangsters as well as various segments of the dominant American culture. He contrasted the random violence of ordinary citizens with also random generosity among the small-time gangsters who suffer from broken hearts and prosper from breaking laws. The humor of Runyon's depiction helped make the gangsters part of the popular American tradition, an extension of the Western gunslinger who had been romanticized previously.

The brief newspaper columns, poems, and short stories are too numerous to summarize individually. Therefore, the collected editions are discussed by topic and theme within a generally chronological sequence. The first three chapters include the early short stories written between 1907 and 1912. Collected last, they have some literary interest in themselves although they bear slight resemblance to the later Broadway tales. The newspaper columns about fictional people and events recollected from this early Western phase demonstrate more aspects of Runyon's later writing style.

Chapters 4 and 5 overlap the time sequence of the newspaper columns. Runyon's newspaper reporting, however, is considered from the early sports columns to later collections of news stories, columns, and short features. Runyon's poetry is also treated as a dimension of his newswriting skill as a featured humorist. As the general format remained the same from early to late, however, the three editions of his poems are discussed together. Finally, Chapters 6 through 9 consider the style of language and humor in the short stories as well as the social satire with which Runyon compared the dominant American society and hoodlum subculture. Runyon's literary accomplishments are evaluated in themselves and as an extension of the humorous writings of such Western predecessors as Mark Twain and A. H. Lewis. Although of a lesser order, he ranks with James Thurber and Ring Lardner because of his distinctive writing style and commentary on various aspects of the American society.

Patricia Ward D'Itri

*Michigan State University*

# Acknowledgments

A myriad of publications kept Damon Runyon's fiction readily available through the early 1960s. I am particularly indebted to Doubleday and Company for permission to quote from *More Guys and Dolls*, originally published by Garden City Books in 1951, and *The Damon Runyon Omnibus* published by the Sun Dial Press, 1944. Other publishers to whom I am indebted are the J. B. Lippincott Company, *Trials and Other Tribulations*, 1947, and *Runyon First and Last*, 1949; Stackpole Sons, *My Old Man*, 1939; Somerset Books, *In Our Town*, 1946; Whittlesey House, McGraw-Hill Book Company, *Short Takes: Readers' Choice of the Best Columns of America's Favorite Newspaperman*, 1946; and Permabooks, *Poems for Men*, 1951.

I would also like to express my appreciation for Edwin P. Hoyt's comprehensive biography, *A Gentleman of Broadway*, Little, Brown and Company, 1964; and Jean Wagner's critical analysis of the short fiction, *Runyonese: The Mind and Craft of Damon Runyon*, Stechert-Hafner, 1965. My thanks extend to Dorothy Moore, who, as executive director of the Damon Runyon–Walter Winchell Cancer Fund, allowed me to examine relevant materials, and to her successor, D. W. Walsh, who kindly extended permission to publish the photograph of Runyon and to quote from Walter Winchell's papers. I am also indebted to Helen Hyres, the current owner of Runyon's birthplace in Manhattan, Kansas, and to Holly Dodds, librarian for the city of Pueblo, Colorado, for their interest and assistance.

Locally, I appreciate the advice and encouragement of Professor David D. Anderson of the Department of American Thought and Language and Professor Emeritus Russell B. Nye of the Department of English at Michigan State University. My thanks are inadequate to reflect the boundless effort expended on my behalf by Interlibrary

Loan Librarian Walter W. Burinski and Clerk Michael Eric Bennett to obtain many of the source materials. I am further obliged to Janet Gassman and Judith Ecker for their perceptive editing and critical insights as well as to Rose McCowan and Terry Waters for assistance in editing as well as typing the manuscript. Most of all, I am grateful for the ongoing support and encouragement of my spouse, Frank M. D'Itri.

Of course all errors and ambiguities are my own.

### Elegy

That which interested him
became significant and
amplified in the daily press.
And that which interested him
was almost perversely
entertaining; murder trials,
touts and tarts, the small
fry of unorganized crime;
the sports heroes of an
overstated century; and the
politics of parades.

He was the god-father of
reportage, T.V.'s talking heads.
He prepared us for dandies
as newsmen, sit-com literature,
and the trivialization of
national life.
Damon Runyon (1880–1946)

by Judith Ecker

# Chronology

1880    Alfred Damon Runyan born October 8, 1880, to Alfred Lee Runyan, editor of the *Manhattan Enterprise*, and Libbie J. Damon Runyan in Manhattan, Kansas.

1887    Family moved to Pueblo, Colorado. Alfred Lee Runyan hired as a typesetter for the *Pueblo Chieftain*.

1889    Left alone with father after Mrs. Runyan died.

1893    Formal education terminated at Hinsdale Elementary School, sixth grade. Employed as an errand boy for local newspapers. Two stories published in the *Pueblo Colorado Advertiser*, then under the temporary editorship of Alfred Lee Runyan.

1895    Hired as a reporter for the *Pueblo Evening Press*.

1898    Enlisted in the 13th Minnesota Volunteers. Wrote for *Manila Freedom* and the *Soldiers' Letter*.

1900    Mustered out of the army and reportedly lived as a hobo for six months. Reported for the *Pueblo Chieftain* and then several other small Colorado newspapers. Name change to Runyon allegedly inspired by a printer's error.

1904    *Collier's Magazine* published poem, "Song of the Bullet."

1906    Reported sports for the *San Francisco Post* and then the *Rocky Mountain News*. Reporting extended to crime, politics, and business.

1907    First short story published in a national magazine. Appeared with caricaturist Doc Bird Finch at county fairs and other local events to promote the *Rocky Mountain News*.

1910    Moved to New York and wrote plots for Charles Van Loan.

1911    Hired as a sports reporter for William Randolph Hearst's *New York American*. Married Ellen Egan, society editor for the *Rocky Mountain News*. *The Tents of Trouble*, a book of verses, published. First name deleted by sports editor Harry Cashman, leaving the by-line Damon Runyon.

1912 *Rhymes of the Firing Line,* a second book of verses, published.

1913 Featured as a humorist in the *New York American.*

1914 Assigned a daily column, "The Mornin's Mornin." Daughter, Mary Elaine, born.

1916 First syndicated by the Hearst newspaper chain as General Black Jack Pershing's forces pursued the troops led by Francisco Villa back into Mexico. A. Mugg introduced in the daily column.

1918 Assigned to Europe as a war correspondent. Son, Damon Runyon, Jr., born.

1919 Signed a new contract with King Features and International News Service, both Hearst affiliates. First biographical series on boxer Jack Dempsey published in the *New York American.*

1921 Second biographical series of columns published on Jack Dempsey, world heavyweight boxing champion.

1926 Arthur "Bugs" Baer, Ring Lardner, and Damon Runyon suspend writing Sunday features in contract dispute.

1929 The first Broadway story, "Romance in the Roaring Forties," published in *Cosmopolitan Magazine.* Detective stories parodied in newspaper series, "Confessions of a Detective."

1931 *Guys and Dolls,* collected edition of Broadway stories, published. Ellen Egan Runyon died.

1932 Married Patrice Amati.

1933 Film version of "Madame La Gimp," *Lady for a Day,* won four academy awards. Ultimately, sixteen short stories and one play were adapted for movies.

1934 *Blue Plate Special,* collected edition of Broadway stories.

1935 *Money From Home,* collected edition of Broadway stories. *A Slight Case of Murder,* a play written with Howard Lindsay, produced on Broadway.

1937 *London Evening Standard* serialized a number of Broadway stories. In London Runyonese became a popular but controversial local dialect.

1938 *Take It Easy,* collection of Broadway stories.

1939   *My Old Man*, columns of opinions by a mythical father.

1940   *My Wife Ethel*, columns narrated by Joe Turp.

1942   Produced *The Big Street*, a movie based on "Little Pinks."

1944   *Runyon a la Carte*, collection of Broadway stories. Cancer of the throat diagnosed and larynx removed.

1946   *In Our Town*, collection of satirical character sketches. *Short Takes*, sampler of newspaper columns. Divorced by Patrice Amati Runyon. Died December 10. Ashes scattered over New York City.

1947   Damon Runyon Memorial Cancer Fund established by friends.

1950   Musical comedy *Guys and Dolls* presented on Broadway.

*Chapter One*

# Newspaperman and Author

## Background

Damon Runyon's childhood is most noteworthy in that his widowed father allowed him wide experience in the streets and newspaper offices while requiring minimal formal education. Born Alfred Damon Runyan on October 8, 1880, in Manhattan, Kansas, he was the first child and only son of Alfred Lee Runyan, a temperamental newspaper editor, and Libbie J. Damon. The family moved several times as Runyan Senior engaged in a series of unsuccessful business partnerships before they finally settled in Pueblo, Colorado. Then financially drained, Runyan took a job as a journeyman printer on the *Pueblo Chieftain*. Libbie Damon died of tuberculosis soon after, and their three daughters were sent to live with her family in Abilene, Kansas. The father and son shared a room at the Mount Pleasant Boarding House and later a shack in the infamous Pepper Sauce Bottoms.

Al Runyan soon followed his father into the newspaper business, at thirteen running errands, and by fifteen becoming a reporter in his own right. During this period his name underwent its first change. Reportedly a printer's error produced Runyon with an "o" instead of an "a." Runyon liked the change and decided to keep it. After he moved to New York, an editor also struck out Alfred and left the famous by-line Damon Runyon. Some stories, however, had appeared without the then-fashionable three-name by-line even while Runyon still worked as a newspaperman in Denver.

Runyon also imitated his father in weaving fantastic tales to embroider upon an already colorful life. As Al Runyan told about fighting Indians during a brief tour of duty as a clerk with Custer's army in 1868, Al Runyon, Jr., enlisted soon after the *Maine* was blown up in Havana Harbor and later also elaborated upon his experiences in the Philippines. Although he was not shipped abroad until after the battle of Manila, Runyon later wrote a stirring eye-witness account. Birth records also belie the claim that he enlisted at fourteen and was the youngest soldier in the Spanish-American War. Rather, out of vanity and advancing years, Runyon later claimed four years less than his actual age, a fabrication still per-petuated on a plaque in front of the house where he was born at 400 Osage Street in Manhattan, Kansas.

Nor do the War Department records substantiate Runyon's claim that he was wounded twice and spent six months in Peking training Chinese and American recruits after the other soldiers came home, although this fabricated experience also became part of his auto-biography.[1] It now seems more likely that Runyon was discharged with the others at the Presidio in San Francisco and celebrated until his money ran out. At that time he either worked for a local news-paper or joined the hoboes and began to learn about life on the road. Then or later, Runyon rode the rods and became acquainted with Kid Swift, who instructed him in the life of the hobo and taught him hobo terminology; at least so the story went.

When Runyon returned to Colorado in 1900, he worked on several small newspapers such as the *In-It Daily* of Glenwood Springs, the *Pueblo Chieftain*, and the *Colorado Springs Gazette*. *Collier's Magazine* published his poem "The Song of the Bullet" in 1904. Runyon later claimed he was hired by the *Denver Post* and fired by editor Joe Ward in 1905. This newspaper, however, has no record of his ever having worked there. When Runyon landed a job with the *San Francisco Post*, he again missed the big moment. Despite later descriptions of his efforts to rescue cholera victims after the earthquake and fire, apparently this heroism was also imaginary, insofar as fellow *Post* employees could substan-tiate his employment record.

Runyon quit the *San Francisco Post* when he was denied the job of sports editor and went back to Denver to work for the *Rocky Mountain News*. A versatile reporter who covered everything from sports to business news and court trials, Runyon published some of his poems in the *News*; and soon his short fiction also was being accepted by national magazines. His first published short story, "Two Men Named Collins," appeared in *Reader Magazine* in 1907. By 1910 Runyon was a seasoned, thirty-year-old newspaperman who was ready to follow predecessors like Bat Masterson and Charles Van Loan to fame and fortune in New York. At Van Loan's recommendation Runyon was hired as a sports reporter on the *New York American*. He was first assigned to cover the New York Giants but quickly progressed to become one of Hearst's highest-paid reporters and columnists.

Whether or not he actually produced the over 90 million published words with which he was credited will probably remain an undisputed contention, as most of them remain uncollected. They are scattered through the daily columns and Sunday features in the decaying pages of the *Rocky Mountain News, New York American, Daily Mirror,* and *Journal American,* the last three Hearst publications. What is certain is that Runyon filled column after column with news reports, editorial opinions, anecdotes, vignettes, short features, and poems. They range from objective news reporting to highly subjective editorials with some short fiction interspersed, particularly in the Sunday features. Although other newsmen and fans admired his colorful and individualistic accounts of events at the ballpark, these columns were strictly ephemeral and now attract only the most dedicated Runyon fans or occasional students of journalism.

### Author

Beginning with "Romance in the Roaring Forties," published in *Cosmopolitan Magazine* in July 1929, Runyon also wrote short stories to make money; and his audience read them to be entertained. Both got what they wanted out of the bargain. By the time events surrounding Black Thursday, October 24, 1929, brought economic chaos to much of the country, Runyon had a standing offer to produce Broadway tales for publication. A steadily wider audience of fans waited for each new magazine story and published collection in Runyon's heyday, the 1930s and 1940s.

He appealed to the mass audience of magazines like *Collier's* and the *Saturday Evening Post* that flourished and were at the height of their circulation before the advent of television. During the Great Depression, when people thought very carefully about how they spent their nickels and dimes, especially for entertainment, and through the subsequent tension of World War II, the name Damon Runyon was a household word.

Approximately eighty stories were published individually and then were collected in numerous editions beginning with *Guys and Dolls* in 1931. It was followed by *Blue Plate Special* in 1934 and *Money From Home* in 1935, the same year that the play written by Runyon and Howard Lindsay, *A Slight Case of Murder*, was produced on Broadway. The first three editions of short stories were combined in *The Damon Runyon Omnibus*, published in 1939. Two other volumes of short stories, *Take It Easy* and *Runyon a la Carte*, were collected with the remainder of his stories in *More Guys and Dolls*, published in 1951. These two volumes include all of his Broadway stories. *Runyon First and Last*, published in 1949, contains some early short stories as well as a selection of my-old-hometown-out-West vignettes and his last two Broadway stories, "Blonde Mink" and "Big Boy Blues." Runyon's reputation as a popular writer of short fiction is based primarily on these stories. The distinctive writing style that incorporated the present tense and Runyonese slang drew a portrait of the small-time hoodlums that inhabit Broadway.

The popularity of the short stories was reinforced by film adaptations. Runyon had already sold one unpublished short story, "The Geezer," to Universal Pictures for movie adaptation in 1927 before his first Broadway story was published. Then Columbia Pictures purchased "Madame La Gimp" in 1932; and the movie *Lady for a Day*, released in 1933, won Academy Awards for star May Robson,

the director, and the screenplay writers. Similarly, the film version
of "Little Miss Marker" had already introduced Shirley Temple to
the American public before the story was published in the second
collected edition, *Blue Plate Special*. Thus, Runyon's literary reception was closely associated with the movie adaptations as well
as with his fame as a newspaper reporter.

In the 1930s Runyon's stories were so popular for movie adaptation that one Hollywood agent maintained that Runyon "has only
to say 'Oh,' and a film company will buy it."[2] Perhaps this was
because Runyon shared the viewers' standards of excellence. According to friends, not only did he have a passion for motion pictures, but "the worse they are, the better Damon likes them."[3]
Walter Winchell contended that Runyon was able to entertain
such a vast segment of the American public because "Damon was
as western as a bronco—as southern as corn pone—and as tartly New
England as cranberry sauce.... Added up—it means he was as
American as apple pie—and just as simple."[4]

This popularity encouraged the publication of collected editions
of some of Runyon's columns as well. In 1939 *My Old Man* and
*My Wife Ethel* were published, followed by *Short Takes* in 1946.
This sampler of columns written from early to late was not as well
received as a collection of the best of Runyon's court reporting, five
trials and one Senate subcommittee hearing, published as *Trials
and Other Tribulations* shortly after his death. All of the anthologies
of short stories and most of the columns were published in Great
Britain as well, and some of them were also translated into foreign
languages. Before the end of his life Runyon claimed to be the most
anthologized American writer.

His poetry would never have brought Runyon recognition other
than for the laughs generated when he rhymed sports stories or
eulogized the fighting men during wars. Like the doggerel composed by Robert Service, it provoked a certain amount of uninten-
tional mirth as well; and Runyon did not list the two volumes
published in 1911 and 1912, *The Tents of Trouble* and *Rhymes of
the Firing Line*, among his later publications. Nonetheless, a new
edition, *Poems for Men*, was published after his death; and it

brought some respectful tributes, particularly for poems that had become accepted as part of the common American heritage.

Walter Winchell was a famous radio broadcaster and newspaper columnist with his own distinctive style and flair for drama when his close friend died of cancer on December 10, 1946. Winchell's spontaneous radio appeal for funds to fight that disease generated a flood of contributions. Thousands of dollars poured in immediately, and the total was eventually millions. The Damon Runyon Memorial Cancer Fund was quickly organized, with a board of directors chosen from among his close friends. They later told stories of tight-mouthed characters who talked like those Runyon portrayed, if they talked at all, as they dumped brown paper bags full of money on the desk at the Damon Runyon Cancer Fund Office. After Winchell died of the same disease in 1972, it was renamed the Damon Runyon–Walter Winchell Cancer Fund. It probably will remain an enduring memorial to both newspapermen.

Runyon continues to be most frequently recalled as a newspaperman, often in the memoirs of colleagues like Irving S. Cobb or well-known offspring like Ring Lardner, Jr. The famous Runyonese appears only in an occasional parody or tribute by an aging newspaper columnist. Critics, however, have increasingly attempted to evaluate the larger currents of popular American literature as well as the writings of the literary elite. In this framework, the enormous popularity of Damon Runyon's Broadway stories in the 1930s and 1940s makes it apparent that he suited contemporary tastes in entertaining the mass audience. Therefore, he warrants critical attention in terms of social currents and humor during two major American upheavals, the Great Depression, especially the early period that included Prohibition, and World War II. His short stories and character sketches juxtapose the gangster subculture against the larger society to demonstrate one dimension of popular humor in the 1930s. They also represent a phase in the development of the short story, part of the transition from western regional literature to more sophisticated and psychologically probing fiction.

## Chapter Two

# Runyon First and Last

## Overview

For the audience who read his short stories in popular magazines and anthologies, Damon Runyon was and still is identified with a small section of Broadway. The mystique of New York City's Great White Way was also enhanced by the stories of colorful hoodlums and hangers-on that Runyon portrayed with warmth and familiarity. Whatever recognition he achieved as an author of fiction was due primarily to the Broadway tales written between 1929 and 1946.

Contrary to the popular myth fostered by Walter Winchell and other friends, however, the famous Runyonese format by no means sprang forth in its mature form with the first Broadway story. Rather, it culminated a long apprenticeship in the fiction-writing craft that began with the early short stories published in major magazines between 1907 and 1912, before and shortly after he left Colorado for New York. Some of these uneven and experimental early stories would never have been collected but for the author's subsequent fame and enormous popularity. They have some literary interest in themselves and as forerunners of his later writing style, however.

Clark Kinnaird's *Runyon First and Last* (1949) includes several of these short stories. They show an uneven quality and style, an experimental approach wherein Runyon tested various narrative formats, points of view, and devices for creating tone, humor, and dialect. The tales seem quite stilted, especially when told by an omniscient narrator. Without the famous Runyonese slang, tag expressions, and present tense, only occasional flashes of humor are reminiscent of the Broadway stories. Runyon adopted some stock literary characters and plots as well as drawing from his own western culture, particularly the former pioneers, Denver politics, current news, and his experiences in the military and among hoboes. The best of these early stories reflect the western frontier humor of the tall tales.

While innovative by comparison with the later stories, even Runyon's early short stories, sketches, and vignettes were drawn from older tales and newspaper accounts as well as from individuals. He followed an established format, refurbishing characters and plots from literature as well as life, particularly the local-color fiction and humor of the frontier, a genre that had passed its zenith by 1900. Despite its influence, Runyon never attempted to limit himself to a regional or local-color orientation. In fact, the early subject matter ranged more widely than the later stories. Nonetheless, he followed a tradition of American humor that had begun when the earliest distinctively American character, the Yankee, was first delineated in *Poor Richard's Almanac* (1732–1758).[1]

Runyon had assimilated the burlesque style handed down by such western frontier humorists as A. B. Longstreet, W. T. Thompson, J. J. Hooper, and G. W. Harris, whose *Sut Lovingood* was published in the *Overland Monthly* in 1867, two years after Mark Twain's "The Celebrated Jumping Frog of Calaveras County" and a year before Bret Harte's "The Luck of Roaring Camp." These two short stories mark the flowering of the local-color tradition. This regional literature flourished from the end of the Civil War to the turn of the century. Harte and particularly Twain and Alfred Henry Lewis influenced many aspects of Runyon's style and humor, especially the character sketches and vignettes in the my-old-hometown-out-West columns.

Runyon had little to do with the efforts of more serious writers to assimilate local-color concepts into fiction with a more penetrating psychological orientation. For others, the environmental conditioning of thought became more organically integrated as a background setting for serious stories. As the cultural milieu evolved, the concepts of local color were further broadened, ultimately becoming a different literary genre after the turn of the century. Instead, in a second line of descent the older, more limited local-color tradition continued in the dime novels about the West and among writers like Runyon who did not seek a depth of coordination between psychology and environment. His character sketches and vignettes maintained the local individuality of village life in my old hometown out West and then merged into the formula plots of the Broadway short stories in which authentic language was combined with stylized literary expressions to form Runyonese.

Critical recognition of this background evolved slowly because Runyon had not been identified with followers of the regional school of local-color writing before his early stories were collected. In fact, two years before *Runyon First and Last* was published, Svend Riemer contended that "nobody, to be sure, has been daring enough to affiliate a writer like Damon Runyon with the proponents of literary regionalism." Nonetheless, Riemer then presented an elaborate theory that Runyon was a new breed of urbanist whose regionalism arose out of "a symbolic presentation of new and pertinent mass experiences" in the way mood and description were captured in plot, language, and sentence structure.[2] No one expanded this viewpoint because the early stories in *Runyon First and Last* led reviewers back to the western regional local-color influences on Runyon, especially from Mark Twain and Bret Harte.

Before that, when collected editions of the Broadway stories were reviewed, critics saw reflections of Rudyard Kipling and Charles Dickens as well as O. Henry. Despite Runyon's experimentation with various writing styles, however, in retrospect it appears that Mark Twain was his single most outstanding literary mentor, just as Ernest Hemingway noted the debt of all subsequent American authors to Twain in *The Green Hills of Africa*. "All modern American literature comes from one book by Mark Twain called 'Huckleberry Finn.' If you read it, you must stop where Nigger Jim is stolen from the boys. That is the real end. The rest is just cheating. But it's the best book we've had. All American writing comes from that. There was nothing before. There has been nothing as good since."[3] Runyon was among the scores of imitators who created a similar narrator. Many of his tales are told as monologues sometimes with identical themes, plots, and cynical attitude toward life.

Undoubtedly, Runyon adopted much from Mark Twain as the Western humorist's perspective was exhibited in *Tom Sawyer*. But he was more influenced by Twain's social satire in *Huck Finn*. As a boy, no doubt Runyon saw parallels between himself and the imaginative Tom Sawyer as well as the motherless Huck Finn. Like Huck he roamed virtually without restraint along the Arkansas instead of the Mississippi River. As a teenager when Runyon became a reporter, like Huck Finn, his objectivity was heightened by the outsider's perspective. From this critical vantage point he observed the hypocrisy of so-called respectable values just as Huck Finn sees that the lovely crockery basket of fruit "warn't real" because you could see "where pieces had chipped off and showed the white chalk or whatever it was underneath."[4]

As Runyon grew up in a cultural milieu not unlike the one that produced Twain, he formed a similar viewpoint. Very early Runyon must have adopted a goal much like Twain's credo: "the deriding of shams, the exposure of pretentious falsities, the laughing of stupid superstitions out of existence." Both authors derive humor by stating painful situations euphemistically, by exaggeration and irreverence, by exuberance, tall tales, and the comedy of hilarious situations. Frequently, there is an air of innocence and surprise, suddenness in turns of expression, metaphors, and conceits. Much humor is derived from the language, folk speech, and incongruity of learned and vernacular, puns, malapropisms, and misquotations of the Bible or classics.[5]

Overall, Runyon was substantially influenced by a number of his fellow western writers, Mark Twain most notably because his work affected many others; A. H. Lewis more than Bret Harte because Runyon also borrowed more of his specific stylistic features as well as plots. A. H. Lewis was one of the more immediate literary resources reflected in the columns about my old hometown out West that were written after Runyon was established at the *New York American* but not when the earlier short stories were written.

### The Early Tales

The underdogs and underworld society are usually defended even in Runyon's early stories about criminals and hoboes, colorful characters on the fringe of society and frequently in its jails. Runyon, however, had not yet perfected his style of defusing the violence and fear with the humor that enabled his later readers to laugh at the Broadway characters. In the later stories, their behavior is justified by the rationale that "what they do is the best they can" when they commit larceny, murder, or lesser crimes such as hustling bets at the racetracks. The code of ethics, however, is similar throughout the early and late fiction. The so-called law-abiding citizens are often as dishonest and brutal as the lawbreakers although they have the appearance of goodness, and the law's reinforcement more often protects them from penalties. Thus, a hint of Runyon's later social rebellion is apparent as good and evil are sometimes reversed among those designated to uphold the law and those who more often disobey it. His code of morality is based on individual ethics rather than social position and, in fact, the rebels are more apt to engage in genuine good deeds, if only for a short time, under unusual circumstances, and in contrast to their customary behavior. Only infrequently foreshadowing Runyon's later cynical humor and antisocial perspective, they more often play on emotions like fear, sentimentality, and nostalgia.

Runyon's humor was generally derived from circumstances of plot or linguistic contrasts, sometimes understatement, elevated language, or localisms and grammatical errors. Although his ear was more tuned to the prospect of getting a laugh than conveying an accurate representation of character and situation, in the early stories Runyon often exhibits a more accurate ear for regional dialect than he does in the Broadway stories. He did not use the tags of highly stylized speech such as "no little and quite some" that attracted the popular audience and repelled critics in later years. Runyon did incorporate slang and regional expressions although without the familiar "which is a way of saying" that often defined terms in the later stories. Instead, he simply inserted the meanings of words between dashes, as in these examples from "The Informal Execution of Soupbone Pew." "We had jungled up—camped— . . . and was boiling our soup—nitroglycerine—from Dynamite."[5]

More loosely plotted than the Broadway tales, the stories have a natural if rambling evolution without the carefully forced twist at the end that later reminded critics of O. Henry. The plots are sufficiently structured to be fairly predictable, however; and Runyon very early tended to repeat any formula that would sell, as evidenced by the similar plots of "As Between Friends" and "The Breeze Kid's Big Tear-Off." Both stories are told by a hobo narrator who describes the effects of a system under which the sheriff usually sentences the hoboes to ten days in jail when they need a place to stay. Then they voluntarily serve the time or not depending on whether the weather improves. The system also benefits the sheriff because he collects fees according to the number of prisoners in his cells.

Whereas these stories sparkle with zest and humor, the tone ranges from crude to somber in others; but it is usually relatively consistent. The mood is somber when violence and fear prevail in stories of human abuse and deception like "The Informal Execution of Soupbone Pew." It is told by another hobo, Chicago Red, much as Dream Street Rose later tells the narrator her story at Mindy's. Both the earlier and later stories are about brutality that provokes retaliation. As Rose kills the man who wronged her, Chicago Red recalls that the Laughing Jag in the adjoining cell had helped the hoboes kill the infamous Soupbone Pew, a tough railroad brakeman who had turned on his former hobo associates.

Sometimes the setting is a framework from which earlier events are recalled, just as the narrator of the later Broadway tales is often in Mindy's or some other restaurant or speakeasy. The early stories are often set in jails but may range as far as a barge adrift in the Philippine Sea. Not being anchored to one locale, Runyon was more concerned with the interactions of characters than the details of physical setting. Only the stories narrated by Private Hanks give a sense of fictional community, a forerunner of the Broadway stories

that are identified by one place but extend to a larger community
wherein the narrator maintains continuity by describing his interactions with other characters.

Glimpses of Runyon's later writing style and sense of humor are
most prevalent in two of these stories about the army and militia.
In "The Defense of Strikerville" combat veterans join the Colorado
militia as strikebreakers because they are not yet ready to reenlist
and face their comrades' ridicule back in the barracks at Fort Logan.
With the promise of earning "$2.00 and found," Hanks describes
with great gusto how they helped put down "the turrible rebellion
in the Coal Creek District." The temporary militiamen of Company
C make friends with the strikers who were driven from their homes
and forced to camp in tents during the bitter winter. Upon hearing
that Company H is off duty and posing as a drunken mob with
orders to drive the strikers out, C Troop arranges to be on patrol.
Then they help the strikers beat back the invaders with a hail of
rock-filled snowballs. Of course, the women are credited with the
victory.

In another story Private Hanks is back in the barracks at Fort
Logan, Colorado, when he recalls Fat Fallon, the lieutenant who
commanded B Troop "back in them days when the war business was
doing well over in the islands." The infantry had been ordered to
attack some villages by land as the cavalry advanced from the sea.
They were set adrift on a barge, however, when the tow line to the
side-wheeler separated in a storm. In a manner reminiscent of Tom
Sawyer, the cavalrymen while away the time playing pirate, using
terms like "shivering our timbers" and "dashing our toplights." "We
figured some on making Barnes walk the plank because he kicked
about tearing his shirt, but we finally compromised on making him
sit in the bow for two hours to represent the figurehead."

At night they hang jack-o'-lanterns over the side so they will be
visible to the side-wheeler. Then they practice their football cheers
in preparation for challenging "those college dubs in the volunteers." In the morning they run aground and learn that the insur-
gents were scared off during the night when a spirit ship carrying

screaming devils cruised along the shore. As the narrator keeps many secrets in the later Broadway tales, Fat Fallon never tells the general why they encountered no enemy opposition.

Another theme Runyon emphasized was the difference between appearance and reality, the need to grapple with contemporary life without romantic illusions or nostalgia for the past. "My Father" deals with efforts of second-generation residents to honor the pioneers, making the classic mistake of doing so while some of these venerable souls were still around to recall and perhaps exaggerate the hardships of pioneer life. As "My Father" bemoans the lost pioneer spirit, Clark Kinnaird called this story a valediction to Runyon's father and the pioneers, a symbolic representation of the changes in American life. This fictional tribute describes an aging Denver pioneer under the thumb of a socialite daughter-in-law who "came into the world when pioneerism had become a sort of misdemeanor, so far as six-pistols and wild Indians are concerned."

The father escapes from his daughter-in-law's household to attend a pioneers' reunion; but his son and wife, Ellen, follow him to Trinity, Colorado, where the Daughters of the Revolution invite her to dedicate a museum to the Spanish explorers. In Trinity the banker son of "Still Bill" is shocked at the terror and respect that his father invokes among the other former pioneers. In the morning the street is empty and the buildings are crowded with fearful people as his father rampages up and down screaming threats and brandishing his pistol. Ellen hastily appears in kimono and hair curlers when she hears that his antics may postpone the dedication of the museum. Followed by anxious onlookers, she pursues the old pioneer into the Blue Moose Saloon; and Runyon's nervous narrator describes the scene in an elevated style reminiscent of that of an earlier American novelist, Charles Brockden Brown.

Imagine my feelings! My beloved wife, unappreciative of the danger attached to an eruption of twenty years of repressed pioneerial fervor, mindful only of the jeopardy of social standing, had flung herself headlong into the arms of Peril.

And my beloved father was Peril!

About me pressed the faces of the people, gray with apprehension, each head bent toward the door of the Blue Moose in a listening attitude.

Shortly I should have plunged through those doors regardless of consequences; shortly I should have rushed to my obvious duty.[6]

But all are saved as Ellen leads "the recently howling wolf and snake in the grass" out of the saloon by the ear. Ignoring his pleas, she gives his favorite notched pistol to a passing youngster. Ironically, later that day she pays high tribute to the Spanish explorers and American pioneers.

Overall, the few flashes of Runyon's future writing style in these early short stories are primarily demonstrated in the humorous descriptions, reactions, and expressions of Private Hanks and the hobo narrator of "As Between Friends." The acceptance of an outsider's status and violence as a common method of achieving revenge also are frequent themes in Runyon's fiction from first to last. At the same time, however, many of these stories and others as yet uncollected have a somber, humorless mood quite unlike the famous style that began to emerge in his poetry and then the columns for the *New York American*.

## My Old Hometown Out West

**Background.** Three groups of anecdotes and character sketches —Grandpap and Grandmaw, My Old Home Town, and Young Squirts—were also included in *Runyon First and Last*. They were written after Runyon had developed a reputation as a humorist and had advanced from sports reporter to columnist on the *New York American*. First introduced as a correspondent to the column in 1916, A. Mugg later became the narrator through whose viewpoint Runyon commented on current news and sporting events, frequently by comparison with an event recalled from my old hometown out West. Between 1916 and 1926 Runyon often expressed an opinion on the editorial page and then developed the same idea in a more anecdotal recounting through the perspective of My Old Man or A. Mugg. Complete with plot and dialogue, these vignettes foreshadow Runyon's later Broadway stories more than the earlier short stories did because of their cynical attitude and mode of achieving humor as well as the use of the present tense, slang, and some of the tag expressions that later became famous Runyonese trademarks. The short vignettes often had twists at the end and a format that was extended into the more involved plots of the later Broadway tales. Thus, they reveal a significant stylistic shift away from the early stories.

Filled with sometimes nostalgic and often cynical recollections, ostensibly of Pueblo, Colorado, these columns were actually tales gathered from many sources. Narrated by A. Mugg in the present tense, events and their recollection are merged to render the concept of time essentially irrelevant. Without a framework such as the later setting of Mindy's or other restaurants or speakeasies, A. Mugg merges the narrative's action and description in a monologue that recalls his youthful adventures with the Young Squirts or stories he heard from others, particularly Grandpap or Grandmaw Mugg.

The same tone of distant amusement, cynicism, and an underlying sense of futility at the prospect of altering human nature is maintained whether the narrator talks about someone "in his pots," meaning drunk and able to recover, "potted" with bullets that render his illness terminal, or women who "take dead aim" at men they want to marry. Goodness and honor are portrayed as something of a novelty in a world where baser impulses generally prevail. Human beings falls in love and out of it, reform, and then return to their usual larcenous ways. They are generally motivated by greed, brutality, drunkenness, or a desire to defraud one another whether by gambling, playing a practical joke, cuckolding other men, or stealing their cattle. Vindictiveness is a prevalent quality along with the tendency to exaggerate one's own abilities and virtues while berating others. The narrator's role, like Mark Twain's credo, is to deride and expose shams, again as a minor character who is more onlooker than participant in most cases.

Larceny and deceit often lead to lawlessness and violence among the so-called respectable citizens in my old hometown out West just as among the later Broadway gangsters. Their cruelty is most frequently directed toward minorities including women, sheep ranchers, strangers, Mexicans, Indians, and Chinese. Citizens with money, generally bankers or gamblers, are accorded dignity and respect regardless of their characters, which are usually unworthy. Some status is also extended to those with physical strength and contentious dispositions, but the gun was recognized as an "old equalizer" that enabled weaker members to even the score long before Runyon coined that term in the Broadway tales.

The Indians and pioneers both come in for a major share of abuse. Like the earlier short story "My Father," when Grandpap Mugg tries to recall and embellish the old pioneer spirit by describing a big battle with the Indians, Grandmaw Mugg interrupts to say it was only four Indians and they were chased off by Missus Wintergreen who threw hot water at them so they would not wake baby Ella May. Grandpap "doesn't like Injuns for snicking arrows in the old days," and continues to resent them long after they "go about their business, or get knocked off by the soldiers. . . . In fact, when I am a young squirt, the only Indian I ever see back in my old home town is the wooden one in front of Lloyd's cigar store, and Jack Dunlavy, the cigarmaker, is generally leaning up against it with his pots on, especially on pay nights."

When asked if Indians are patient, Grandpap replies that Job Dunn is more so and tells the story of Dumb Dan. Job owes Dumb Dan $4.00 for a sheep, and Dan stands in front of Job's cigar store waiting for payment until he dies. Dan had been there so long that Job misses him and has a statue carved to replace him.

Besides the obvious biblical pun on patient Job being dunned, this story of the origins of the wooden Indian demonstrates the way Runyon adapted events, settings, or older plots to his particular locale. As Washington Irving adapted "Rip Van Winkle" and other stories from their original German setting to the Catskill Mountains, Runyon moved some of these tales farther West. Like Rip Van Winkle, Zeb Griscom flees from his wife. Then the search party sent to hunt for him also disappears. Before long, Grandmaw Mugg finds them all partying in the Greenhorn Mountains and forces them to return home.

Like Mark Twain, Runyon drew many examples of the effect of
greed on human behavior and the status accorded citizens who have
money by those who do not, regardless of how the wealth was obtained. "Christmas Revenge" bears many parallels with Twain's
"The Man That Corrupted Hadleyburg." After Swede Sam Suden-
burg is run out of my old hometown as a no-account guy, he strikes
it rich on a mining claim. Nobody objects or is suspicious when
he wants to give the town a big Christmas celebration. Local people
greet him warmly, but their hypocrisy is rewarded by disaster. After
Sam presents the girls with bicycles and the boys with .22-caliber
rifles, no one is safe on the streets. The townspeople retaliate by
passing an ordinance that forbids both Sam and public Christmas
trees within the county lines for ten years.

The local prejudices against Mexicans, Chinese, and especially
the Native People of the area demonstrate a vicious form of humor
and the hypocrisy of the local citizens. For example, Mexicans bear
the brunt of Tut Tuttle's practical joke when he steals the rooster
weather vane off the courthouse and buries it where they play a
cruel form of polo, racing horses past buried chickens and grabbing
their heads off. After a Mexican named Romero falls off his horse
trying to grab the head off the weather vane, he nicks Tuttle's ear
with a knife. Then Tuttle has to buy the courthouse a new weather
vane as "no one has the heart to ask Romero for the other one back."
This tale foreshadows the later "Sense of Humor" in which human
beings are murdered as practical jokes. Also like the Broadway tales,
the explanation avoids the real issue. Tuttle is afraid to ask Romero
for the weather vane back, just as in "The Lily of St. Pierre" the
narrator suggests that Jack O'Hearts might really have shot Louie
the Lug to take his place in their barbershop quartet instead of as
revenge for Louie's treatment of Lily.

As Runyon's early story "Fat Fallon" demonstrates influences
from Mark Twain such as the cavalrymen whiling away their time
aboard a barge by playing pirates, this background is also apparent
in five Boo Gang sketches that Clark Kinnaird strung together in
an anecdotal narrative. Like Mark Twain's juveniles, the Boo Gang
frequent a cave where they pretend to be the Jesse James gang,

Captain Kidd's pirates, or Kit Carson's scouts. They capture Chief Yellow Hammer, who is really Dirty Sam, a Navajo, and "not much of a terror except maybe to the free lunch at the Arkansas Hall Saloon." They tie Sam up, pretend to burn him at the stake, and then roll him into Mill Ditch to put out the fire. After Marshal Pat Dillon rescues Sam, the town has to care for him for the rest of his life.

Just as Mark Twain's Huck Finn and Jim discover bank robbers in a mysterious house, the Young Squirts see Mr. Harrison bury something at the Hemingway house, supposedly the most haunted house in the area. Returning with Grandpap Mugg, they also uncover stolen money. In another incident like "Tragedy in the Graveyard," a chapter in *The Adventures of Tom Sawyer*, young Mugg overhears Clinton P. Markweather try to kill Jeff Dunn for "fooling with his wife." No one is hurt, however, because Mrs. Markweather had removed the bullets from both guns. Upon hearing this Grandpap Mugg offers the Young Squirts only the explanation that women are very strange. The circumstances are reversed in the Broadway story "Social Error" when Basil Valentine tries to look like a hero by shooting Handsome Jack Maddigan with blank bullets. Red Henry substitutes real ones, and Miss Midgie Muldoon is wounded while trying to protect Handsome Jack. This story also has a forerunner in A. H. Lewis's *The Sunset Trail*, in which the Wild Rose is shot while trying to protect Bat Masterson.

**Humor.** Virtually devoid of literary analogies or references, these tales draw their humor from a range of sources such as applying the terminology of legal activities to those that are illegal and vice-versa, and by symbolic names and slang expressions as well as understatement and exaggeration. Much of the humor is derived from contrasting diverse elements in a situation and from championing larcenous and violent individuals rather than the respectable but condescending citizens.

These columns often include Runyon's familiar set expressions to define slang terms such as "clev which is a way of saying a knife." In some cases one slang term defines another: "and are always weighing in the old sacks about it, which is a way of saying they

are always knocking it." Although they have a quite different tone,
in some respects the tag expressions resemble those repeated by
Frank Norris in *The Octopus*, such as "Keast of the ranch of the
same name." Such general statements can simplify description, as
when Runyon offered a few details and then abbreviated the remainder to explain what a picnic is. "A picnic is a proposition where
people go to a grove of a Sunday, with lunches of sandwiches and
cold chicken, *and all this and all that*, and also with plenty of beer,
and have a wonderful time. Or anyway that is what a picnic is back
in my old home town out West." In another simplification, Saw-
tooth Samuelson's larcenous record is summarized by noting that
he "puts in his time stealing other people's cattle, and one thing and
another."

Humor is often also derived by exaggerating the magnitude of the
problem or focusing on a peripheral issue. When Old Simp takes
all of the clothing at the picnic of the Bartenders' Association and
they have to stay an extra day in the woods, "the suffering among
them is terrible, as the beer gives out during the night." In addition,
the townspeople suffer because the bars are closed two days in a row.

Western colloquialisms predominate in a variety of expressions
and sentence structures. During an attempted bank robbery "all of
a sudden from every roof and window along the street comes a-boil-
ing bullets." Then the two Karrick boys, "who never have no great
deal of sand anyway, stick their rowels into their horses and away
they go." Bad Pete, however, is "as game a guy as ever steps in shoe
leather." In contrast, after Old Simp steals their clothes, the naked
bartenders "cuss" and take "smacks" at one another until Marshal
Pat Dillon gets them "out of their pickle." In addition, errors of
grammar add humor and reflect the limited schooling in my old
hometown out West. For instance, the men are usually "too scared
of their wives to mistreat her." And Highpockets says, "I bid five
bucks on them feet" at a box social where he is tricked into outbid-
ding Buck Wiggens to sit with Miss Marthy Sprowls.

Conformity to literary codes also encourages the inclusion of
western euphemisms. It snows "like Billy-be-danged," and Jack

Reeves "is well known to one and all as a guy who loves to raise plenty of Cain." The western origin of an expression is noted as the narrator describes a big, rough character "who will shoot you setting as they say back in my old home town out West." And the winds "knock everything which is not tied down stem-winding." Other clichés also reinforce the local aura such as "put on the feed bag," "by no means stuck up," "no use crying over spilt milk," "his middle name is Trouble," and "before you can say Jack Robinson." Swede Sam Sudenberg shows that his heart "is in the right place" when he gives the children guns and bicycles for Christmas. Then the townspeople see "what a terrible man he is at heart."

Much humor is derived from exaggeration or understatement. After Rawhide's father raises him to be so tough he can sleep outdoors in blizzards, he dies of pneumonia contracted while walking a colicky baby in his living room. And an iron chicken is "especially still" because it is anchored in the ground with a long iron picket pin so "the chances are that a team of horses cannot pull it out." This unnecessary emphasis is reminiscent of expressions used by A. H. Lewis, such as when the sheriff is found "undeniably dead."

Some of the exaggerations are as preposterous as Mark Twain's tall tales. Hickory Slim is so old that he was a two-year-old about the same time that Pike's Peak was a hole in the ground, and Mrs. Sam Tolbert is so thin that "you can hardly see her when she turns sideways." The townspeople consider passing a law that would limit whiskers to two feet in length when Jonas Walk's almost reach his knees. And G. H. Pendleton's limited generosity is fatally taxed when his "heart swells up to the size of a pea and busts."

The character sketches and yarns included in *Runyon First and Last* show the most direct link between Runyon's western influences and the later Broadway stories in the style of the latter and the subject matter of the former. In addition, the evolution of his short-story format is evident in the contrast between the earliest and last two tales. Until 1949 Runyon's fiction had seemed virtually unchangeable as he had adhered to one successful formula in the Broadway stories published in 1929 and afterwards. Two other volumes of columns, however, *My Old Man* and *In Our Town*, show different aspects of Runyon's style with subject matter mostly in the my-old-hometown-out-West setting.

## Chapter Three

# My Old Man and In Our Town

## Introduction

Among the collected editions of Runyon's newspaper columns, the vignettes in *Runyon First and Last* (1949) are most similar to the style of the Broadway tales, but as Runyon perfected his present-tense format with the extensive use of slang and tag expressions, he also developed a variety of other less successful writing styles. The collected columns in *My Old Man* (1939), some of which were republished in the "Our Old Man" segment of *Short Takes* (1946), and the *In Our Town* (1946) character sketches, demonstrates Runyon's versatility compared with the uneven early short stories and the highly stylized Broadway fiction. Both the *My Old Man* and *In Our Town* collections have distinctive and relatively consistent styles and perspectives. Just as these collections represent two examples of the diverse writing styles that Runyon perfected during the 1920s, they also show how his subject matter shifted from western to eastern and how his role as social critic was expressed. Like Edgar Lee Masters, Sherwood Anderson, Sinclair Lewis, and especially Mark Twain, Runyon joined those who fled from the village to seek their fortunes and build their literary reputations in no small part by scornfully looking back on what they left behind. Each tried to "do his share in lifting at least a corner of the veil of sanctimoniousness and self-satisfaction behind which moneyed respectability was hiding its corruptions, perversions, and tragedies."[1]

While Runyon was reminiscing about the greed and hypocrisy in my old hometown out West for the Sunday features of the *New York American*, the citizens of Sauk Centre, Minnesota, were reeling with dismay at the fictional portraits Sinclair Lewis drew in *Main Street* and *Babbitt*; however, whereas Lewis's novels were published, reviewed, and attracted wide public attention and critical acclaim, Runyon's vignettes were published in the newspaper one at a time; and they often had a rollicking, humorous tone that overlaid the caustic comments. Therefore, the readers laughed instead of being offended at his indictments of the American social system. Perhaps what Runyon later called "a half-boob air" deprived him of the castigation that would also have constituted a form of recognition for his role as a self-appointed social critic. Like Sinclair Lewis, Runyon "was impaling types common to nearly every town or neighborhood, but his lance thrusts went unnoticed because he was not supposed to be thrusting lances."[2] By the time *My Old Man* (1939) and especially *In Our Town* (1946) and *Runyon First and Last* (1949) were published, Runyon was a famous author, proudly claimed by Pueblo and Denver as well as New York, but still disregarded as a social critic. This was probably because of his humor and the fact that he wrote small pieces for an out-of-town newspaper. Nor did he associate with the local intelligentsia or explain his social views and writing techniques on the lecture circuit. No doubt all of these contributed to maintaining Runyon's reputation as a humorist without the additional aura of social critic.

Runyon edited these volumes of columns and emphasized certain aspects of his social orientation by the selection and order of presentation. For instance, one column was published in three collected editions. Titled "On Good Turns" in *My Old Man* and *Short Takes*, the same column appears at the beginning of *In Our Town* under the title "Our Old Man." Although the format reflected the *My Old Man* columns, Runyon must have wanted to emphasize the motto "Never Blame the Booster for What the Sucker Does." This column is the only one to appear in all of the collections, although a number of others were published a second time in *Short Takes*, and all were originally published in the *New York*

*American* newspaper. The slogan is repeated after several examples in which the person trying to con someone else is victimized instead. For instance, Poker Joe is fleeced by a stranger My Old Man brought to his poker room. The tables are turned, however, when a friend named Chris sells My Old Man fake gold stock and then mails him a copy of his own motto.[3]

In some cases, the opinions expressed in *My Old Man* and the *In Our Town* character sketches represent different interpretations of the same idea. Generally, the further the tales are distanced from editorial opinion, the more vivid they are. An example of this is the column "On Doctors" in *My Old Man* and "Dr. Davenport," a character sketch in *In Our Town*. Both columns state how little credit doctors receive for saving people's lives and how reluctant the patients are to pay their bills after they are cured, even though they would have given all of their wealth when they were still ill: ". . . but after some doctor pulled them back from the dark abyss and they got to walking around again, they were not willing to pay even a minute percentage of their holdings."

My Old Man notes that doctors continue to see patients who do not pay and sometimes even risk their health to do so. Doctors are strapped for money because they rarely ask a patient in physical stress to "lay a little something on the line in advance." Nonetheless, physicians are expected to dress well, have nice tools, and maintain a tranquil, reassuring mood. Thus, My Old Man concludes that a law ought to be passed to insure that doctors will be paid, thereby giving them the peace of mind to discharge their functions properly.

Unlike this well-intentioned recommendation for socialized medicine, in the *In Our Town* version Dr. Davenport makes the same point more directly by taking the law into his own hands. Because Dr. Davenport was independently wealthy, he never billed anyone who was financially pressed. Consequently, the other people seldom paid him either. When Dr. Davenport lost his money in the Depression and tried to collect some of the overdue bills, people were unsympathetic and still refused to pay even when he was almost starving. "He went around looking seedy, and forlorn, and most people said it served him right for being such a bad businessman and not attending to his affairs better."

When Dr. Davenport finally borrowed a gun from a friend on the police force and threatened to blow the heads off citizens who owed him money if they did not pay, he collected $6,876.70 by nightfall. Then Dr. Davenport was able to eat his first square meal in nine months.

. . . but he never had much standing in Our Town afterward, as the better class would not patronize him.

They said a doctor who expected to get paid for his services must be crazy. The seventy cents Dr. Davenport collected from Mrs. Gabe Wheeler, whose husband, Gabe Wheeler, had borrowed the money from Dr. Davenport seven years before to buy rough-on-rats, which Gabe took himself.

Mrs. Wheeler always felt grateful to Dr. Davenport for that, even though she had neglected to pay back the money.[4]

The narrator is essentially the same in both versions, a minor character who recounts events and people's reactions. Having only one speaker describe and sometimes respond to the actions, however, makes the *In Our Town* version more concise than when he repeats My Old Man's opinions. The action is faster and the humor emerges more quickly and directly along with a large measure of Runyon's antisocial isolation and cynicism.

### My Old Man

My Old Man is one of the most frequently depicted characters in Runyon's newspaper columns. The nostalgic and mild-mannered homespun philosopher with just a touch of larceny and malice is the central character in the collected edition of columns entitled *My Old Man*. This culminated the fictional representations that began with "My Father," a short story about the old pioneers that was published in 1911, the year Runyon's father died. This fictional character is more rebellious, resembling Grandpap Mugg, who is also a former pioneer trying to reclaim the western frontier spirit. Like Mark Twain's characters, My Old Man has "an almost preternatural shrewdness thinly veiled under the assumption of simplicity."[5]

Runyon's later recollections of his father must have been torn between the tall stories and jokes that Runyan senior told as he held court at the Arkansas Hall and Greenlight saloons and the efforts of the harried widower to discipline his son on the run between the saloon and a job as printer on the *Pueblo Chieftain*. Certainly Runyon acquired more of his education from his father and associates in the saloons and newspaper office than from his occasional excursions to Hinsdale Elementary School, which he abandoned entirely after the sixth grade. Later Runyon recalled that his father could quote from Shakespeare and Milton by the yard. He also could discuss with equal skill such diverse issues as women's suffrage, the the silver question, and the odds against filling an inside straight.

By the time Runyon was a columnist and humorist for the *New York American*, the stories told by his father, others heard and read, and his own opinions formed a composite background for a variety of columns with widely diverse subjects. Old yarns were often refurbished; and other tall tales were set in the framework of recollections of My Old Man, Grandpap and Grandmaw Mugg, and the Young Squirts. Many of the as yet uncollected columns follow the format of having a twist at the end and contain the Runyonese present tense and tag expressions that later became famous in the Broadway stories. Often a contemporary news event sparks A. Mugg to recall something that happened in my old hometown out West. In other vignettes events of the fictional past are simply recounted without contemporary references.

The somewhat bland My Old Man columns probably would not have been collected in 1939, much less republished as part of *Short Takes* in 1946, but for Runyon's well-established reputation as a newspaper columnist and writer of short fiction. Whereas many of the uncollected columns are frolicsome vignettes in the same style as the Broadway short stories, at the height of its popularity Runyon sacrificed this writing style in the collected edition. Instead, the dialogue of the *My Old Man* collection is generally in the past tense. The sense of immediacy is lost and the prose is deadened by the seemingly endless repetition of "my old man said." Nonetheless, a few flashes of Runyon's cynicism enliven the vignettes. They sometimes end with a twist that reinforces a point set forth at the beginning or on a related but less significant matter. While some of the slang expressions are included, the linguistic color is more often provided by local western expressions or clichés.

Apparently Runyon dispensed with a proven, popular format to focus attention on the social views presented secondhand by A. Mugg, the primary narrator who recollects opinions ostensibly expressed by My Old Man. Whereas A. Mugg occasionally interjects his own interpretation, more often all of the characters' actions and reactions are funneled through My Old Man's viewpoint, thus homogenizing the action into a single perspective that is duller than a variety of individual responses would have been.

Runyon may also have sacrificed his usual style to soften the image of My Old Man. He confronts the weaknesses in others tolerantly while trying to maintain his own illusions intact. The perspective is uneven as My Old Man alternates between a disconcerting innocence, or at least its appearance, and a cynical viewpoint on reality. Often he reverses or makes fun of traditional beliefs held by the established but often hypocritical society such as "our best citizens'" lip-service faith in the Protestant work ethic. He also debunks an assortment of old saws such as "Early to bed and early to rise makes a man healthy, wealthy, and wise." My Old Man contends, instead, that this advice might make some men hollow chested and nervous.

In most of the columns, My Old Man is represented as a homespun philosopher of the cracker-barrel school of wisdom often depicted on such television programs as "Hee Haw" and "The Beverly Hillbillies." He is an outgrowth of the tradition followed by Will Rogers, Artemus Ward, and earlier predecessors in folk humor and wisdom that can be traced back to the shrewd but quickly parodied Yankee trader. In the role of a generous commentator with a clear insight into other people's values, My Old Man too humbly acknowledges his own weaknesses while discounting those of others. This mellow tolerance sets a tone more reminiscent of Pollyanna than the shrewd, antisocial, tongue-in-cheek cynicism for which Runyon was famous. When My Old Man speaks as a western version of Everyman, however, he expresses opinions that reflect common denominators of the human condition revealed through ordinary people and circumstances. In this sense he demonstrates one of Runyon's most basic themes, the everyday foibles of ordinary men.

The flashes of humor and insight are farther apart in the *My Old Man* columns than in the Broadway tales or the character sketches of *In Our Town*. Nonetheless, some aspects of Runyon's famous style are evident in the cynical reflections on human nature and some infrequent but familiar expressions. For instance, My Old Man objects to the way preachers "boost" those "shaking off this mortal coil." He does not think the act of dying "rounded up a fellow who had been petty and mean." Therefore, if the preacher couldn't truthfully say something good about "defunct citizens," he should at least be noncommittal.

Runyon's analogies are often drawn from everyday incidents or common expressions. In "On Growing Old" My Old Man recalls how he became aware that "the years were nailing him to the mast." He also describes a fellow who is "as homespun as corncobs." Another time he recalls an elderly person who is "up in the paints," an expression derived from a gambling game called Faro Bank in which high cards are called paint cards. Even accounts of gambling by buying gold-mining stocks bring out Runyonese exaggerations such as "a roll of money that could have choked four horses" and "as good as wheat in the bin."

Socially accepted professions invoke more than a believable measure of respect from the superficially optimistic old man. He offers such unremarkable contentions as that preachers are usually honest. By his logic, they would have to be to stay in that low-paid profession for more than five years. Therefore, My Old Man said that "if he had a great raft of money" he would give annuities so preachers would be able "to go belting right and left through the land" and not have to be biased in favor of influential parishioners. Similarly, most doctors are skillful and do not deserve to be kept waiting for their money. Moreover, "he said whatever a doctor got, it was seldom enough." My Old Man also feels sorry for bankers because they cannot complain about business and so join in with the boys.

Food and digestion are important in these columns as in the Broadway tales. My Old Man said he quit hating because it was bad for his nerves and stomach, and for his disposition, too. Food is the basis for some homespun observations such as that it tastes better when one is hungry, and My Old Man fondly recalls a hunk of prairie dog cooked over a brushwood fire. As taste reflects cultivation, he sings the praises of hotcakes. He errs on the side of being too truthful in telling a man what a terrible cook his wife is, but humor is created by reversing the expected when My Old Man notes that "he had spent most of his life dodging pie like his mother used to make."

Disillusionments in the war between the sexes frequently intensify My Old Man's gallantry as well as cynicism. Unlike the *In Our Town* sketches, violence is underplayed as he notes that "our Western womanhood of those days were generally so hale and hearty that wife-beating was a rather precarious enterprise." Nonetheless, he thinks happily married couples could teach others how to be successful in marriage, but the cost would be exorbitant to distinguish the ones who are truly happily married from those who make false claims.

These brief summaries show some aspects of ordinary human behavior as well as a few unusual incidents that attracted My Old Man's comments. Opinions interlaced with anecdotes reflect the usual format of Runyon's daily columns more than the better-organized vignettes of *In Our Town*.

### In Our Town

Whereas the *My Old Man* columns generally express a moderate, even tolerant outlook on his own and other people's foibles, the

*In Our Town* vignettes often have a bitter outlook and enough cynicism to suit the audience attracted to Runyon's darker Broadway tales. They most graphically demonstrate Runyon's increasing alienation from the American society both because of the starkness of the negative behavior and its preponderance. The initial critical reception of *In Our Town* (1946) varied widely but was generally favorable, and Runyon reportedly said, "I am astonished at the way they are being received," especially as the same columns had generated little attention when they were originally published in the *New York American*.[6]

Three vignettes—"Lou Louder," "Burge McCall," and "Joe Terrace"—were published in *Collier's Magazine* in 1936. They closely resemble the twenty-seven sketches collected as *In Our Town* a decade later. The first story in the volume, "Our Old Man," had also previously been published as "On Good Turns" in *My Old Man*. The last sketch in this collection also varies somewhat from the remainder. Like "Our Old Man," "Hank Smith" has an anecdotal format that resembles the column that introduced Chelsea McBride in 1919. In this case, veteran Hank Smith describes his wounds, all at the hands of women during various wars. Each event is interspersed with an appropriate line of music.[7]

These sketches are all named after the central character and reveal an incident that dramatically affected him or her, often ending with some kind of twist in the plot. They are all told by a relatively objective third person, a minor character whose local background is demonstrated by his familiarity with the other characters' personalities and histories. He describes what happens to them and their reactions in a simplistic manner that weaves together dialogue, action, and a little description; but he maintains a rather innocent, somewhat distanced perspective. The narrator is a bystander who tells about events in my old hometown out West in the past tense and shifts to the present if the characters move to his street in New York.

Whereas My Old Man derides pretension and exposes hypocrisy with a sham *mea culpa* attitude that the narrator occasionally exposes, in *In Our Town* he makes no attempt to excuse or explain the violence, greed, and hypocrisy that are only occasionally inter-spersed with acts of kindness, generosity, or courage. The conflicts are usually between intimates, often husbands and wives whose social training in morals and ethics is overcome as they succumb to baser impulses. "Our best citizens" have few redeeming virtues and often reflect due cause for Runyon's alienation.

The simplistic narrative style was a format that Runyon had ex-perimented with when he was writing Sunday features for the *New American* in the early 1920s. One of these was a eulogy to Bat Masterson. The old gunslinger turned gambler and then reporter had preceded Runyon to New York and died at his typewriter in 1921. He is introduced in the same manner as the fictional protag-onists of *In Our Town*. "Bat Masterson is dead. The famous West-ern trailblazer and peace officer, of late years a noted sports authority, crossed the Big Divide yesterday."[8] A typical fictional example is the introduction to "Lou Louder." "Lou Louder was a bartender. He tended bar in the Greenlight Saloon. He was tending bar there the night Shalimar Duke was killed. Lou Louder was very tall, and very thin, and very pale. He said he was sent to Our Town by a doctor in Buffalo, N.Y., to die. Lou Louder had t.b."[9]

Although the two Baker boys, Pablita Duke, and her husband all came in the saloon with the intention of killing Lou Louder, Pab-lita Duke killed her husband by mistake, and the two Baker brothers were hanged for the crime. Although they were armed with guns and Duke was killed with a knife, each confessed to save the other after they were arrested, one by the sheriff and the other by the chief of police. "It was all very confusing to the citizens of Our Town when the stories were compared after the funeral." Then Pablita Duke died of pneumonia contracted while meeting a traveling man in a storm, and the intended murder victim was the only one left. The twist at the end relates to the usually ordinary circumstances of Lou Louder's demise.

Lou Louder remarked to Doc Wilcox just before he died that he always felt he had a rather narrow escape that night.

He didn't die of t.b.

He died of old age.

The Chamber of Commerce of Our Town often pointed to Lou Louder during his life as an example of what our climate will do for a man.[10]

On the basis of parallels drawn between "Lou Louder" and Ernest Hemingway's "The Killers," Jean Wagner contended that Runyon attempted to imitate the spare, dramatic precision of this classic short story published in 1927. As both Hemingway and Runyon chose the titles *My Old Man* and *In Our Town*, Wagner saw an additional similarity in the crisp *In Our Town* vignettes that are less cluttered with linguistic tags than the Broadway stories. Wagner attributed this to an attempt by Runyon to develop a terse, matter-of-fact style akin to Hemingway's and very different, at any rate, from Runyon's usual wordiness.[11]

Whether or not Runyon was under his influence, Hemingway made dramatic strides in the development of the short story that Runyon could only admire and emulate in a small way. Both Hemingway and Runyon expressed a cynical attitude toward human nature, and the characters usually became embittered by their experiences. In "The Killers" when the boy, Nick Adams, realizes that Ole Anderson will be killed by the gangsters and he is helpless to prevent it, his perception of the world is altered although George cynically observes that the best thing to do is forget it.

Hemingway builds a psychological climate of tension by means of concise dialogue that expresses the characters' distinctive personalities. The reader's sophisticated cooperation is required to link the small portion of the action that is described with the perspective of what preceded and the inevitable outcome to follow.[12] Whereas the conversation in "The Killers" forces the reader to conceptualize the situation and accompanying behavior, Runyon's reader learns what happens only from the narrator's perspective and is kept away from such direct psychological involvement.

Humor breaks the tension as the action is also disrupted by irrelevant comments or details. In some cases it is derived from the language and in others from the absurdity of situations, the characters' reactions to them, or the juxtaposition of irrelevant details against very important events. For example, the fact that Sid Baker has a gun on his left hip because he is left handed relates to Baker's intention to kill Shalimar Duke. By contrast, the description of perfume from roses growing at the side door of the Greenlight Saloon is followed by the irrelevant observation that this is a strange place for roses to grow, but they were always growing in strange places in Our Town.

Kenneth Payson Kempton contended that readers would willingly accept the effort Hemingway's story requires because of the correspondingly great rewards, except "perhaps those whose lips move when they read." When Runyon's wordy style and contrived plots are compared with Hemingway's sparse and vivid precision, it appears that the teller of yarns may well have intended his convoluted plots for the latter audience. David W. Maurer noted that some of Runyon's characters are those who read only the sports pages and the racing forms and have trouble with them. Runyon also said he did not want to be blamed for the crack "You can't exaggerate the stupidity of the public." In one of his darker moods, however, he concluded, "But the more I see of the world, my good friends, the more I am inclined to the belief maybe the guy who said it had something there."[13]

In Runyon's character sketches the antisocial attitude is quite graphic as the Puritan ethic is frequently reversed. Then the lazy, evil, or incompetent are rewarded. Widely held beliefs are often also refuted, such as the idea that money corrupts and goodness and virtue must win out over evil. Instead, good fortune is as likely to be showered upon the undeserving citizens profiled in *In Our Town* as on those to whom respectability would give a greater claim.

As virtue is not rewarded nor sin penalized, violence may be provoked spontaneously or as an outgrowth of a long-standing hatred. Shootings are common among women as well as men, but the former are also particularly given to using knives and other kitchen equipment to attack their spouses whereas the children arm themselves with rocks. Among men, bank robbers and "our best citizens" all carry firearms, ostensibly for hunting but also to obtain their ends or seek revenge. The issue is usually decided by whoever draws first unless one individual is an exceptionally poor shot or drunker than usual.

Sometimes the distinctive names of male characters have humorous, ironic overtones. For instance, Severance Kake is known locally as Angel, a name that in no way suits his character. The nicknames reflect the men's insider status whereas women are generally excluded from drinking, gambling, and cardplaying in the saloons as well as from festive occasions like the bartenders' annual picnic. Western gallantry accords them a title, but Miss has an ironic edge because the single women strive to be Mrs. until marriage redirects them toward violence and betrayal.

Examples of Runyon's usual slang are decidedly sparse. Among the few, Sam Crable is handcuffed with the "comealongs," and townspeople generally regard Ancil Toombs as "N.G. in spades." More often, linguistic analogies are old clichés, such as "They all raised a terrible row." "Old plugs" describe men instead of horses, and one farm has such poor land that "you couldn't even raise hell on the place."

Nor are tag expressions very common, although Judge Joes had "a few grandchildren here and there." Runyon's characters also reflect their limited education by a few common grammatical errors such as "He could hear good too, unless you asked him for money." The ongoing narrative incorporates dialogue with description in the narrator's pell-mell accounting of events and conversations. Thus, he recalls Miss Blanche Astee's complaint that "she had fooled her best years away with him and look at her now."

Often the portraits reflect a pattern of great cruelty that is mitigated only by his humorous expression. Runyon notes that big men always like little bitsy women, and little men always go for women the size of a first baseman. "This is the way it is in life"; and Samuel Graze, who is "musclebound from the neck up," frequently beats his ninety-pound wife, Magda. Although other citizens said he ought to pick on a woman his size, they do not interfere. Finally, "he gave her a very fine beating and went to bed," whereupon Magda kills him. Then the townspeople marvel that such a small woman could kill such a big man as Samuel. The judge lets her off with a reprimand, "although some thought it was setting a bad example to the other women in Our Town whose husbands like to give them a beating now and then."

Attempts at goodness and understanding commonly are futile or provoke a negative backlash. Newspaper editor Boswell Van Dusen nearly goes broke when he only prints good things. But when he starts printing derogatory news, local people feel obliged to buy advertising space and include him in other financial deals to protect themselves. Similarly, after a burglar is allowed to escape because he pretended to be a poor man trying to augment his allowance from his wife, Officer Lipscomber decides to arrest people first and think about their problems later. Nor is taxi driver Pete Hankins sure honesty is the best policy when he drives all over New York to return a purse to a woman who insulted him earlier. Then she does not even thank him. Apparently she is like the police who "call all taxicab drivers by the same name. It is Hey You."

Many of these character sketches are adaptations of older tales placed in the local environment, and Runyon never claimed they were original. His use of specific details, however, such as references to Hinsdale School and Riverview Cemetery in Pueblo, Colorado, led to some charges of plagiarism. This accusation was raised about the story "Doc Brackett" when it first appeared in the *New York American* and again when it was published as part of *In Our Town* in 1946. Runyon said he had only told the story the way he heard it long before. He said he was glad to have the matter settled when a reader claimed the original was told about a Dr. John Goodfellow by a nineteenth-century Ohio writer, Dr. James Ball Naylor.

In Runyon's version, Doc Brackett remained a bachelor after Miss Elvira Cromwell called off the wedding because he went to care for an ailing Mexican child on the day they planned to marry. She said a man who thought more of a Mexican child than of his own wedding was no good. When he died at age seventy, people talked of putting up a nice tombstone; but no one did anything. Finally, the Mexican family took the sign from the foot of the stairs leading to his office and placed it over his grave. It read: Dr. Brackett, Office Upstairs. Such twists unified the vignettes or made a peripheral point that still gave a sense of conclusion. Reminiscent of O. Henry's style, they became a trademark of the Broadway stories as well.

*Chapter Four*

# Newspaper Reporter

## Background

The journalists' immediate recountings of significant events have never been accorded the dignity and prestige of the more distant and academic historians. In a collection of newspaper accounts entitled *A Treasury of Great Reporting*, however, editors Lewis L. Snyder and Richard B. Morris demonstrate that much remarkable literature has been written under pressure. Noting Matthew Arnold's comment that "journalism is literature in a hurry," the editors include Runyon's news stories with those by other authors who developed their writing skills under the stress of meeting deadlines. Among those who later gained fame by writing fiction were Stephen Crane and Ernest Hemingway as well as Ring Lardner and Rudyard Kipling.[1] Both of the latter were Runyon's colleagues on the *New York American*. During that period Kipling and James Oliver Curwood contributed occasional pieces whereas Lardner's short features ran under Runyon's byline and above those by Arthur "Bugs" Baer for quite some time. Later, Irving S. Cobb replaced Lardner; but Runyon maintained his position as featured humorist over some of the best-known writers of his day, both on his own newspaper and among competitors.

Loyal, flamboyant, and occasionally brilliant, most of all Runyon was prolific. When the tributes of his colleagues were filed, no one disputed Bugs Baer's contention that Runyon could write the other reporters out of the newspaper if he were given a chance.[2] Damon Runyon won the respect of colleagues who regarded him as one of the foremost sports writers as well as a versatile reporter who covered leading news events ranging from politics to murder trials. Runyon wrote classic news stories such as his description of the parade of the battle-scarred 27th Division up Fifth Avenue at the end of World War I. At his death eulogists praised Runyon for not having forsaken his post as a newsman after he achieved fame as a writer of short fiction and success as a movie producer. In fact, Runyon left his own sickbed to cover the funeral of Franklin Delano Roosevelt, his last major news story.[3]

Many of the more flamboyant sportscasters now are television commentators who supplement pictures with live coverage of the action. Like Runyon, however, newspaper reporters still offer extended coverage of sporting events, filing daily columns with interpretations, opinions, and anecdotes. Heywood Hale Broun follows in his father's and Runyon's footsteps with colorful reporting, and Charles Osgood occasionally reports the sports news in rhymed verse, doggerel much like what Runyon occasionally presented in his sports columns. Nonetheless, few newsmen develop such flamboyant styles as those of Runyon and Walter Winchell anymore. Even sports writers are taming what Stanley Woodward called their "unholy jargon."[4]

The pace was more leisurely when Runyon wrote, although he also was influenced by the increasing emphasis on time instead of space that began at the turn of the century. He insisted that columns should be limited to 750 words and chided himself for "windifying" when he exceeded that.[5] Many of his news stories followed the now traditional format, presenting the major facts first and then a detailed exposition in decreasing order of importance. Like all good writers, however, Runyon allowed himself substantial latitude for different approaches. He was especially adept at describing small details and angles that were often overlooked by other reporters. Runyon probably adapted easily to writing fiction because many of his news stories often did not follow a traditional reporting style anyway. Three volumes of columns demonstrate his skill and versatility as a news reporter and columnist: *Short Takes, Trials and Other Tribulations,* and *My Wife Ethel.*

### Short Takes

By the time *Short Takes* was published in 1946, Runyon's column was syndicated in over one hundred newspapers and reportedly had a daily readership of over 10 million people. Even with a large popular following and the sympathy of colleagues who knew Runyon was terminally ill with cancer, however, the collected vignettes, anecdotes, and miscellaneous trivia were not substantial enough to warrant acclaim in a collected edition. The reviewers were decidedly cool.

Murray Schumach said the material was well organized for the benefit of commuters and subway patrons, but he recommended it only for Runyon's most ardent admirers "of which there are more than somewhat."[6] *Newsweek* reprinted much of the column about death coming to visit Runyon before his laryngectomy in 1944, but the reviewer only noted the general content of *Short Takes* without critical comment.[7] *Short Takes*, however, received one remarkable review, the one written by Runyon himself.

On the same day that news of Runyon's divorce from his second wife was published, the columnist reviewed his own *Short Takes*. Runyon took the occasion to review his career as well as this sampler of columns written from early to late. The column was widely quoted in other reviews, subsequent obituaries, and other news stories about his life and work. Runyon concluded that *Short Takes* contains "enough gummed-up syntax to patch hell a mile." Thus, he could not commend it for its literary qualities. Bitterness predominates as Runyon says: "But as a study in the art of carrying water on both shoulders, of sophistry, of writing with tongue-in-cheek, and of intellectual dishonesty, I think it has no superior since the beginning of time. . . ."[8]

Runyon did contend, however, that he was more of a social critic than people generally realized. Saying things with a half-boob air, he was able to get ideas out of his system on the wrongs of the world, although his ability to convey thoughts by indirection made it appear that he was not personally responsible for what he said, thus undercutting its significance. In his own defense Runyon said that his social comments were allowed if passed off as humor whereas they would have been erased if said in a more serious tone. At the end of his life, Runyon was his own most severe critic. In passing judgment on himself, Runyon proclaimed that he had always been a rebel at heart; but he had lacked the moral courage to stand up for his beliefs. "I tell you Runyon has subtlety, but it is the considered opinion of this reviewer that it is a great pity the guy did not remain a rebel out-and-out even at the cost of a good position at the feed trough."

Whereas he satirized those who tried to recapture the past in his early short stories, the collection of columns largely written later in his life bespeaks, in many instances, the reminiscences of a gentler, more sentimental Runyon: a dying man with more perspective on the present through the events and particularly the people that he recalled from former times. The critical columns were generally written at an earlier stage of life. While A. Mugg is not directly represented, some of the columns from *My Old Man* are republished as "Our Old Man" in this sampler that also includes some of the Turp columns under the subtitle "Mr. Joe Turp Writes." Some of these had appeared in *My Wife Ethel*, and all had been published in the daily newspaper at one time or another.

Unlike the *My Old Man, In Our Town,* and *My Wife Ethel* collections, *Short Takes* does not maintain a single point of view, theme, or format. Each section includes Runyon's columns on a particular topic, such as autobiographical notes, sports, Broadway and Hollywood characters, animals, domestic issues, his illness, and even some fairy tales. The diversity of writing styles, formats, and opinions in this collection effectively demonstrates Runyon's versatility. Except for columns reprinted from previous collections, most of them are from the later years when Runyon was an intimate of the famous as well as the notorious, an established author and movie producer, no longer eager to shock the reader or anger his friends.

Although Runyon had not completely lost his cynical bite even in the last columns, he usually said something good as well as something amusing about the stars and lesser lights with whom he associated on Broadway and in Hollywood. More the man about town

than the hard- or even medium-boiled reporter, Runyon paid tribute
to Babe Didrikson, the athlete; Mabel Norman, the actress; George
Burns, the comedian; and Max Weinberg, a Broadway character
otherwise known as Sledgy, who ran a quickie photograph studio
where people posed with their heads sticking out from behind paint-
ings of comic costumes. Even those who were better known no longer
grace the society news, much less the front page. Thus Runyon's
bland and sometimes fawning accounts of their activities are often
less interesting than the fictional profiles published as *In Our Town*
the same year.

Acknowledging himself to be a master of trivia in one column,
Runyon proved the claim in many more. Often the columns are
composed of a loose collection of opinions, observations, or brief anecdotes, sometimes witty opinions about dining, wives, or pets as
well as sports and gambling. The columns about his illness, his bed,
and his fantasy of an encounter with Death are more painfully immediate. Some of the columns, however, also demonstrate Runyon's
best style, notably "A Great Man Passes By," the column on Franklin Delano Roosevelt's funeral. It is in a league with his description
of the parade of the 27th Division upon its return to New York in
1919. And the formats are quite similar, alternating between a description of the event and the onlooker's reactions, in this case a
father reminiscing about FDR to his son.

Other columns express Runyon's cynical views on wealth and
human nature. He tells a young "punk" to get the money and repeatedly describes wealth as his standard of success. Runyon cautions that money is not everything, "It is only 99 percent of everything." By the same token, he suggests that the in-betweens, Mr.
and Mrs. Mugg, are really worse off than the rich or the poor because they have no buffer from calamity.[9] In another column, Runyon quotes the Bible in support of his contention that it is better
not to trust anyone, a viewpoint also voiced in a "My Old Man"
column and at least implicit in much else that Runyon wrote.

In other cases Runyon seems to talk down to his readers. With
regard to his literary style and subject matter, Runyon describes
himself as an intellectual Robin Hood. "I steal from the rich in

wisdom and give it to the poor." After listing famous writers from whom he borrowed, including the orator Socrates, he acknowledges that "Sometimes I wonder if youse appreciate me."

While the style varies widely even in columns written near the same time, the present tense and his usual slang appear only infrequently in this collection. Among the few examples, with rhyming slang he describes a pain in the Darby Kelly (belly). In a play on words a section about gambling is entitled "The Bettor Life," although the overall theme is reminiscent of the poem "All Hawse Players *Must* Die Broke." One column demonstrates this as he recounts a bet that he will return from the dead. Inappropriately mixed terminology also creates a humorous allusion to "inmates of the movie capitol" in another example of Runyon's famous style.

He also refutes some of the myths he helped create and repeats the hobo stories that he had included in his biographical columns about Jack Dempsey more than two decades earlier. "And yet I have seen the day when I magnified a few little jaunts of my own into a regular hobo career, though of course I was never any more a real 'bo than one of the Rockefeller kids." Another column recalls the legend of the "Diamond Jo," reportedly "a hobo-proof train with a standing offer of $500 to any 'bo who could ride 'er from Malvern Junction into Hot Springs, Arkansas." The legend sometimes placed the winner in the water tank or the cowcatcher. Runyon also said he never believed the old yarn about a coupling-pin being dangled to knock a hobo off the rods under a train "though I put it in all seriousness in my story of Jack Dempsey's hobo days as having happened to Jack and in fact I think Jack imagined it did. But you see, long before I ever knew of Dempsey I heard the story as having happened on railroads other than the Santa Fe."

Runyon notes that it had been fashionable for writers "to put themselves away" as former hoboes, presumably in imitation of Jack London, who was supposed to have been an "all around rough-and-tumble gee, and a lot of anemic, hollow-chested pen pushers, journalists and story writers tried to pattern their lives after his." Runyon again recounts the story of A No. 1, the greatest of the hoboes, and recalls monikers such as "Cincy Skin," "Peoria Shine," and "Chey-

enne Red." They were characters he had written about in early
short stories and poems. He also speculates that he could not see
why the railroads were so stingy about transporting hoboes who
occupied space they did not otherwise use.

Runyon's playful side is displayed in a few columns subtitled
"For Children Only," such as "The Tale of Sneaky the Germ," another about a Paul Bunyon–like soldier named "Algernon," and two
tales about Louie, the hard-drinking stork who delivers babies. One
of these columns relates how Sherman Billingsley's Stork Club got
its name because he gave Louie permanent quarters. Another is
about Phooey Pigeon, who tried to take over Louie's territory; a
gangster in birdland.

"Rope Tricks" more closely resembles the Broadway stories. A
dispatch about auctioning off the furnishings of the old United
States Hotel in Saratoga Springs reminds Runyon of the ropes
supplied instead of fire escapes when the hotel was built 119 years
earlier. A horse player named Frankie Buzzsaw once tried to hang
himself with one of these ropes when he was broke and discouraged.
By then the rope was over a century old, and "you know few ropes
that age can stand such a strain." The rope parted, and Frankie fell
on his bookie, who then chased him "plumb to Mechanicsville."
Thus, Frankie lost out on the chance to bet on a horse that paid
100 to 1. The narrator concludes that "I never could understand
why he did not go ahead with his suicide idea in some other form
when he got the result but the last I heard, Frankie is still alive and
quite hearty only he hates ropes."

Runyon carried his public prudery and objections to offensive
language to the end of his life. In "Passing the Word Along," written after his larynx was removed, he notes that "most American
humor is in bad taste and growing worse under the present vogue
for the suggestive and the downright obscene in the spoken and
written word. But even the suggestive and the obscene is not as un-
kind as the humor dealing with bodily affliction."

The range of Runyon's tones is also demonstrated in *Short Takes*.
The anguished cry of "Why me?" brings out the shock and bewil-
derment of learning about his terminal illness. "It becomes a pulse

beat—'Why me? Why me? Why me?'" Runyon notes that "I, too, am just a poor mugg groping in the dark" as he retells the story of Job in Runyonese. ". . . Sabeans copped all of Job's oxen and asses . . . but Satan again appeared . . . and the Lord started boosting Job for holding fast to his integrity . . . but finally Job let out quite a beef . . . and cursed the day he was born."

After the greed, fame, suffering, and fairy tales, the columns about Joe and Ethel Turp of Brooklyn lend a soothing touch of normalcy. The book concludes on an optimistic, even sentimental note with a column on the founding of the United Nations, one of the best filed in the name of Joe Turp. Joe describes Ethel's visit with Mrs. Tyler, who mourns for her dead son and others lost in the war. Willie "had to go all the way from this little corner of Brooklyn to the Philippines to get killed and Jakey Levine to Sicily and Freddy Williams to Germany." As Ethel and Joe recall the wounded and the dead as well as those who grieve, they agree that the same thing could happen to their son Cornelius. Therefore, their hope for better times rests with "the new set-up now that ought to prevent another war if it works the way they hope it will."

This final Turp column and Runyon's description of Franklin Delano Roosevelt's funeral procession are examples of some of his best newspaper writing. They demonstrate the subtlety with which he could play sentimental chords. Many of the columns, however, have little literary value other than to demonstrate his versatility, the range of his interests, and to add a few insights into Runyon's beliefs, background, and attitude toward news reporting.

### Trials and Other Tribulations

High tribute was paid to Damon Runyon's skills as a newspaper reporter when *Trials and Other Tribulations* was published in 1947, a year after his death and some fifteen to twenty years after the daily newspaper accounts of five trials and one Senate subcommittee hearing were originally published in the *New York American* between 1926 and 1933. According to the publisher this book was the last that Runyon planned. In that regard, it is most interesting as a representation of his views on society. The factual, if subjective, chronologically presented collection of trial reports reinforces the social perspective of the Broadway tales and indicates, to some degree, Runyon's social isolation and knowledge of the gangster subculture.

Runyon was no novice at courtroom reporting when the Hall-Mills murder trial began in 1926. He had observed the vagaries of justice, western style, from his earliest newspaper reporting in Pueblo, Colorado. According to Runyon's undoubtedly colored recollection, his first big news story concerned a bandit lynched by a mob of vigilantes. He was hanged from a telegraph pole behind Pueblo's Grand Hotel.[10] As a seventeen-year-old reporter, Runyon saw the thin line between lawman and lawbreaker when the mob first placed the rope around the neck of the district attorney, Miles G. Saunders, before someone recognized the error and the proper culprit was hanged. At least that is the way Runyon told the story.

Fifty years later, in 1946 Runyon reinforced the cynical views formulated by such earlier experiences when he chose and arranged a selection of court and hearing reports for publication. As Runyon's isolation from society was reflected in the early court reports and subsequent Broadway tales, it is given a final twist in *Trials and Other Tribulations.*

Runyon effected a social comment rather than simply showing his eye for drama, detail, and the reactions of individuals partly by which trials were included and which were left out. Among the latter, Runyon had been brave enough to risk unpopularity by defending Fatty Arbuckle publicly. The comedian had outraged public morality by an unsavory scandal when a woman died at a wild party in San Francisco in 1927. The same year, Runyon produced what Gene Fowler said was his only news story turned down in favor of an Associated Press Wire Service report. Convinced that Sacco and Vanzetti were innocent, on the eve of their electrocution Runyon wired a story that began "They're frying Sacco and Vanzetti in the morning." While his fictional tough guys could kill one another on whim or as a practical joke, this lead was too much for newspaper editors to let their readers face over the breakfast table in 1927. Nor did Runyon include his much-acclaimed reports of Bruno Hauptmann's trial for kidnapping the Lindbergh baby.

Rather he chose and edited daily columns of five trials and one Senate hearing that related some clear morals or comments on the American social system. One distinctive theme is the humorous contempt with which Runyon views the upper echelons of society when their hypocrisy is exposed in trials for murder or separate maintenance. In contrast, Runyon was more respectful in references to the dead gambler Arnold Rothstein when George C. McManus was on trial for his murder. And his account of Al Capone's trial for income tax evasion is especially conservative. This is notable in comparison with the accounts of an investigation by a subcommittee of the Senate Committee on Banking and Currency into allegations that J. P. Morgan, the financier, paid no taxes during the years that Capone was accused of paying too little. These two final segments of *Trials and Other Tribulations* in themselves reflect some of Runyon's most cynical views on the American social structure.

The facts of these trials are presented so that good and evil have less relevance than the arbitrary distinctions of social status, especially when reinforced by "a lot of potatoes." Moreover, wealth stolen within the law warrants more respect than the ill-gotten gains by members of the underworld, the same code of ethics often expressed in recollections of my old hometown out West.

By 1926 Runyon's newspaper reporting had become dull and repetitive; but the old sparkle returned in columns about three trials, all the outgrowth of domestic discontent—one request for separate maintenance and two murders of husbands by wives. All had distinguished participants and the hint of adultery, thus virtually assuring a wide audience in both the courtroom and the newspaper. Beginning with the Hall-Mills murder trial, they were all conducted during the six months from early November 1926 to the end of April 1927. Runyon filled columns of the *New York American* with descriptions of the setting, protagonists, and packed galleries.

The theatrical drama of this trilogy, the first three trials in *Trials and Other Tribulations*, was ready material for Runyon's descriptive talents. He understood the prejudices, fears, and interests of the audience for whom he wrote. They wanted to know about such external badges of status as the participants' clothing and automobiles. His careful eye for detail and his subjective reactions pander to the readers' interest in sensationalism. Runyon served as Everyman's eyewitness in the courtroom. The old sports reporter also was very crowd conscious. He bitingly portrays the hordes of people who scrambled for the few spectator seats in the crowded courtroom so they could watch the sordid revelations unfold firsthand. At one point, Runyon recalled the works of a British artist as he remarked that "it seems a pity that old man Hogarth isn't living to depict the crowd scene in the courtroom yesterday."[11] Among the observers were actors with a professional interest, such as Edward G. Robinson, who reportedly based his portrayal of Little Caesar on Al Capone. Others among the curious onlookers were also well known, such as the Marquis of Queensbury, Petrova the ballerina, and songwriter Irving Berlin. Runyon speculated on the endurance of women who waited outside for hours or stood on tiptoe at the back of the room to catch a glimpse of other women charged with killing their husbands, Mrs. Hall or Mrs. Snyder, or at the precocious sixteen-year-old Peaches Browning, who asked separate maintenance from her fifty-two-year-old "Daddy."

Runyon reacted with a range of emotions from overt sentimentality to staged shock, but he generally maintained a relatively subdued tone. The past tense is interspersed with a little sophisticated humor and moments of glee marked by slang such as "getting her into the feathers," "an able two-handed drinker," and what would shock a "medium boiled reporter." Analogies with sporting events convey a circus atmosphere, and sometimes hints and subjective commentary verge on being libelous while the generalizations sound almost inane.

In his first time at bat as a big-time court reporter in the Hall-Mills case, Runyon used many sports analogies to describe a wealthy heiress to the Johnson pharmaceutical fortune as she and her two brothers stood before the bar of justice in a small New Jersey courtroom. They were accused of the murder four years earlier of Mrs. Hall's husband, a minister, along with his choir leader. Their bodies had been found under a crab-apple tree with their love letters scattered over them. Runyon noted that the trial was like a sports event even to the extent that the switchboard used for the Dempsey-Tunny fight had been brought in to enable a local radio station to broadcast the proceedings. Runyon contended that speculators could get a very good price if tickets were sold because the courthouse had very limited seating and the drama "is such a cast as David Belasco might revel in."

The Hall-Mills murder trial had sex and intrigue and even a mystery witness. The "Pig Woman," Mrs. Jane Gibson, was a retired lady bareback rider who claimed she actually saw the murder. Although she was seriously ill, instead of moving the jury to the hospital, she was dramatically carried into the courtroom to give her testimony. Runyon later cynically told a friend that the story would have been improved if she had died right there. As it was, wealth and what Runyon called "Jersey justice" prevailed. The defendants were acquitted.

Runyon adopted a more playful tone and reverted to the old "Dear Reader" format to report the hearing of sixteen-year-old Peaches Browning, who requested legal separation from her fifty-two-year-old "Daddy" in January 1927. The readers' interest was whetted with veiled allusions to the foibles of a man past the "fifty yard line" that could not be described in a family newspaper. "Your Uncle Samuel would bar it from his mails. They are the things that are only put in plays nowadays—the kind of plays that Mayor Jimmy Walker often speaks of censoring." He reported that "Your correspondent's manly cheeks are still suffused with blushes," and Runyon contended that the gods must have guffawed as people almost rioted in their desire to get a peep at the principals in a duel of defamation "as they looked down and watched the earthworms wriggling in the muck heap of a modern-day matrimonial squabble."

Runyon really hit his stride as a trial reporter three months later with his account of what he called "the dumbbell murder," otherwise titled "The Eternal Blonde." Whereas the Hall-Mills case had appeared to be vengeance against the matrimonial wandering of a minister and his choir leader, in this case a corset salesman named

Henry Judd Gray was prevailed upon by "a cold eyed blonde" to lift a sash weight in the murder of her husband, Albert Snyder. As they had already confessed, Runyon was not hesitant to judge even as the trial opened. "It was stupid beyond imagination, and so brutal that the thought of it probably makes many a peaceful, home-loving Long Islander of the Albert Snyder type shiver in his pajamas as he prepares for bed."

With slurs on blondes that went unchallenged then, but now would likely provoke picketing by NOW, WEAL, and blondes of every shade that nature and Clairol could provide, Runyon indicated that any man might fall victim to a blonde; and this one "has blue-green eyes and [is] as chilly looking as an ice cream cone."

In contrast, Runyon gushed sentimentally when the defendant's nine-year-old daughter, Lorraine Snyder, took the stand.

She was, please God, such a fleeting little shadow that one had scarcely stopped gulping over her appearance before she was gone.

She was asked just three questions by Hazleton as she sat in the big witness chair, a wide-brimmed black hat shading her tiny face, her presence there, it seemed to me, a reproach to civilization.

Justice Scudder called the little girl to his side, and she stood looking bravely into his eyes, the saddest, the most tragic little figure, my friends, ever viewed by gods or men.[12]

In other instances, his metaphors provoke laughter that may not always have been intended. "Not much jocularity to Henry Judd Gray now as he shrinks in and out of the court room in Long Island City while the ponderous machinery of the law grinds the sausage of circumstance into links of evidence." According to Runyon, the more nervous listeners concluded at the close of Mrs. Snyder's examination that they should recommend "that hereafter no blonde shall be permitted to purchase a window sash weight without a prescription and that all male suburbanites should cancel their life insurance forthwith and try all the doors before going to bed."

Continuing with sports analogies, Runyon speculated that the sash weight hitting Albert Snyder's head must have sounded like

Babe Ruth hitting a home run. Henry Judd Gray showed the "pop-eyed jurors" how he slugged the sleeping art editor with "a sash-weight stance much like the batting form of Waner of the Pittsburgh Pirates." In this case, the jury members must have felt the blow because both Ruth Brown Snyder and Henry Judd Gray were sentenced to death by electrocution.

The fourth trial, that of George McManus for the murder of Arnold Rothstein, authenticates some of the aspects of the gangsters' language that were widely argued after Runyon's short stories appeared. Runyon admired the gambler and had written with great respect about his stamina as a high roller. Later, Rothstein and an earlier gambler, Herman Rosenthal, were the basis of the fictional character "The Brain," who appears in "A Very Honorable Guy" (1929) and "The Brain Goes Home" (1931).

"Arnold Rothstein's Final Payoff" is particularly interesting as evidence of Runyon's knowledge of the gangster subculture. On the night he was killed, November 4, 1928, Rothstein reportedly was engaged in conversation with Runyon at Lindy's Restaurant. Later the state claimed that the gambler was summoned from Lindy's to pay overdue IOUs given in an earlier high-stakes poker game. If Runyon actually knew anything about the events related to the murder, he never said. Instead, his respect for the underworld code of loyalty is demonstrated in his account of the state's revelation that Rothstein died "game." The gambler had often been heard to remark that "if anyone gets me, they'll burn for it." But as he lay bleeding to death from gunshot wounds in an alley, Arnold Rothstein reverted to type and refused to say who had shot him. "He was no longer the money king, with property scattered all over the Greater City, a big apartment house on fashionable Park Avenue, a Rolls-Royce and a Minerva at his beck and call, and secretaries and servants bowing to him. He was a man of the underworld. And as one of the 'dice hustlers' of the dingy garage lofts, and the 'mobsters' high and low he muttered, 'I won't tell.' A sigh of relief escaped many a chest at those words, you can bet on that."

The authenticity of Runyon's use of the present tense to replicate gangster speech patterns was not challenged until ten years later.

During this trial, which began in New York City on November 19, 1929, however, this usage was dramatically documented. When Prosecuting Attorney Ferdinand Pecora asked how witness Martin Bowe fared in the high-stakes poker game that reportedly caused Rothstein's death, Bowe replied, "I lose." With regards to another player, Meyer Boston, Bowe said, "He wins."

The state of New York had indicted George McManus, Hyman Biller, and two unknowns identified as Richard Roe and John Doe largely on the basis of four liquor glasses in the hotel room where they allegedly played poker the night Rothstein died. Biller left town before they could arrest him, and the other two were never identified. Although the gun was found, this "smoke-pole" could only be traced as far as St. Paul, Minnesota, where it had been purchased. When the state's attorneys failed to prove their contention that Rothstein had been shot in Room 349 of the Park Central Hotel, Judge Nott finally dropped all charges against McManus and the others on the grounds that the state had failed to make a case.

Two years later, Runyon managed to find even less humor in the tax-evasion trial of another gangster acquaintance, Al Capone. Although he had visited Capone and his brother Ralph at their winter fortress on Palm Island between Miami and Miami Beach, they had little opportunity for neighborly interaction after 1932 when Runyon built a house on nearby Hibiscus Island. Capone was confined to a Philadelphia prison in 1930 on a charge of carrying a concealed weapon in the City of Brotherly Love. Soon after he left jail and returned to Chicago, the federal authorities indicted him for nonpayment of income taxes.

The account of Capone's trial has greater significance as a social comment in comparison with the last sequence of news stories in *Trials and Other Tribulations*, "Morgan the Mighty." In May 1933, a year and a half after the Capone trial, the Senate Subcommittee of the United States Senate Committee on Banking and Currency delved into the allegation that J. P. Morgan had not paid his appropriate share of federal income taxes. Whereas the United States Federal Court in Chicago contended that Capone owed approximately $215,000 in taxes on an income of over $1 million for the years 1924 –1929 inclusive, Morgan admitted he paid no income tax at all in 1931 or 1932. He did not remember about 1930. In fact, the twenty partners in the J. Pierpont Morgan firm, many of them supposed to be very wealthy, paid an aggregate income tax of $48,000 in 1930 and none in 1931 and 1932. The footwork was amazing. With a profit of nearly $2,225,000 for only one day, they managed to show a loss of over $21 million for two days. In contrast, United States Attorney George E. Q. Johnson scoffed at testimony that Al Capone had lost $327,000 betting on horses and categorized the defense witnesses who told of these losses as being "so shifty they couldn't look you in the eye."

Both Capone and Morgan were such well-known public figures that they attracted crowds of onlookers and reporters to their trials, and both were supported by teams of lawyers. Among the onlookers a myth had sprung up that the investigation into Capone's taxes began when President Hoover was ignored in a Miami Beach hotel lobby where Capone was being mobbed by hero-worshipers. Similarly, J. P. Morgan had always been annoyed by photographers; and Runyon noted that the "photo grabbers" had a field day taking Morgan's picture in the courtroom, although they were so used to having him try to grab their cameras that they quickly retreated when he made sudden moves. Morgan was so cooperative, however, that he even allowed them to take his picture with a female midget sitting on his lap. She had been sent into the room by a Ringling Brothers Circus press agent. Runyon gleefully described "the midgeting of Mr. Morgan." According to him the members of the Senate subcommittee were greatly annoyed when they heard about it later, "possibly because there are no midgets left to pose on their knees." Then photographers were barred from the caucus room, "although they are scarcely to blame for littering up the place with midgets." Runyon also took this occasion to wax philosophical. "The philosopher may see the midget as occupying toward Mr. Morgan the same relative position now occupied by the proletariat of these United States of America. That is to say, we are all more or less on Mr. Morgan's financial knee. There is this difference between us and the midget, however; Mr. Morgan occasionally bends us over his financial knee, south side uppermost."

At the culmination of this investigation, the senators thanked J. P. Morgan for his cooperation, and in 1934 a Security and Exchange Commission was established to regulate the stock exchanges and the future issue and sale of securities. In contrast, at the conclusion of the government's case against Al Capone, the United States Attorney warned the jury to remember the men and women who pay a tax on incomes over $1,500 a year and contrasted them with Capone, "whom he flayed for evading taxes during 'this time of national deficit.'" United States Attorney George E. Q. Johnson contended that the United States Government has no more important laws to enforce than the revenue laws and concluded that "This case will determine whether any man is above the law." Not surprisingly, Capone was sentenced to eleven years in prison while J. P. Morgan went on to help finance Lend-Lease to Great Britain, France, and Russia during World War II.

While the daily activities of gangsters made front-page news, the readers' interest was sufficient to warrant additional columns of historical information about earlier racketeers. A sequence entitled "From Becker to Rothstein" by John Harkins recalled that one gangland era ended when Gyp the Blood, Dago Frank, Whitey Lewis, and Lefty Louie were executed for the murder of gambler Herman Rosenthal on April 13, 1914. Runyon was the contemporary historian of gangland culture; and he ingratiated himself with the underworld not only by his loyalty, but also by occasionally inserting small bits of information in his column. "'The boys tell me,' he said one day, 'that R. A. T. Tourbillion, otherwise Ratsy, otherwise Don Collins, or Dapper Don who is in stir in New Jersey with plenty of time wrapped around his neck, is there on a dead wrong rap, as they say.'"

Runyon's was the voice of authority, and he corrected the reports of others regarding such things as the gangsters' extravagant funerals. For example, he informed his readers that "The $15,000 caskets you read about in connection with the funerals of rich gangsters cost closer to $2,000 tops." In addition, David W. Maurer recalled the favored status Runyon held with underworld characters. Testifying to Runyon's authentic presentation of the underworld argot, Maurer remembered him sitting at a table in a restaurant going over his stories with underworld characters, unofficial editors who verified their authenticity. According to Maurer, Runyon was one of the favored few who could walk with immunity among them. The gangsters looked out for his well-being. With this background, Runyon's short stories were initially received as authentic representations of Broadway characters and their language. Although subsequent challenges weakened his credibility, Maurer and others have since verified Runyon's reliability as a spokesman for the gangster argot despite some distinctly Runyonesque modifications.

## The Turps

**Newspaper Columns.** When Runyon was singled out from among Hearst's stable of reporters to replace the distinguished Arthur Brisbane as the featured editorial columnist following Brisbane's death in 1937, the occasion was marked by an article on Runyon's newspaper and fiction writing in *News-Week*.[13] Although Brisbane had called Runyon America's greatest reporter, it soon was apparent that his talents were not suited to producing the ponderous and weighty observations on world events that had given Brisbane the nickname "Double Dome" and the honored first column at the top of page one of the *New York American*. Consequently, Runyon was soon back at his usual post recounting the personal foibles and colorful details of the lives of distinguished or notorious citizens.

In the 1930s Runyon hit upon one of his most successful vehicles for expressing his views on mundane daily matters ranging from domestic wars to local politics. In this format, something like Ring Lardner's *You Know Me, Al*, a citizen of Brooklyn named Joe Turp writes to the columnist to describe wife Ethel's witticisms and methods of manipulating her husband, something in the manner of the George Burns and Gracie Allen comedy team. Runyon spoke through the Turps on social and political issues to the end of his life. In addition, two short stories about the Turps were also published, "A Call on the President" in 1937 and "Nothing Happens in Brooklyn" in 1938. They demonstrate Runyon's transition from feature column to short story as the same characters and style are woven into a more complicated plot.

The first collected edition of these columns, *My Wife Ethel*, was published in London in 1939, the same year that *My Old Man* was published in the United States. American editions followed, but the Turps continued to be more popular in Great Britain. *The Turps*, a collected edition of all these columns, was published there in 1951. Edwin P. Hoyt speculated that the Turps were better received by the British, who were interested in the Americans' domestic habits, whereas the Americans themselves were not as enthralled to be reminded of the essential pettiness and insipidity of most domestic relationships. At any rate, an editorial note in this last edition says ten of the letters were "the last fictions written by Runyon. He was on his death bed when he doggedly tapped them out on a portable typewriter."[14]

While all of the columns are from Joe Turp's perspective, the shared domestic interactions give Ethel a much more dominant role than women generally have in Runyon's stories. Ethel initiates things and Joe follows. She picks the fights, and he gets knocked down defending her honor. In a sense, the Turps represent Runyon's interpretation of the lives and opinions of ordinary Americans, the small daily interactions primarily with spouse, family, and neighbors, pondering major events secondhand rather than by direct observation.

The present-tense dialogue flavored with lower-class speech mannerisms communicates that Joe and Ethel are of modest education. Without the underworld terminology and other slang, the language is less startling than that of the Broadway stories.[15] Nonetheless, Runyon tried to capture the pell-mell flow of ordinary conversation recollected in a later narrative. Instead of the usual artificial "he said" and then direct dialogue or a summary by the author, Joe's narrative style is seldom interrupted by internal punctuation. He jumps back and forth from what he "ses" to what Ethel "ses" with an occasional improper use of the negative such as "Ethel ses Joe we got no time for that an' I ses you're right Ethel" or other reflections of lower-class speech patterns. Furthermore, some of the background detail is summarized in the past tense which is woven right in with the present tense dialogue. "By this time Ethel was in front of the building pounding with her fist on one of the boarded-up windows and the cops had stopped shooting and were watching her. Ethel told me afterwards that when she had pounded her fist black and blue Clem Chambers ses who is it?"[16]

In contrast, in the Broadway tales the narrator recounts events and dialogue in the third person and present tense.

Well, naturally nobody will wish to see their Maw under such circumstances, but Big Jule's Maw lives over in West Forty-ninth Street near Eleventh Avenue, and who is living in the very same block but Johnny Brannigan, the strong arm copper, and it is a hundred to one if Big Jule goes nosing around his old neighborhood, Johnny Brannigan will hear of it, and if there is one guy Johnny Brannigan does not care for, it is Big Jule, although they are kids together.[17]

The daily columns in the form of Joe's letters are briefer and have less elaborate plots than the short stories. They could serve as a kind of Everyman's history of the late 1930s and early 1940s as well as a diary of domestic life. Joe and Ethel discuss everything from shaving cream to why Joe Kennedy would not wear short pants to meet the King of England and who might get the lead in the movie version of "Gone With the Wind." As they speculate about whether or not Roosevelt will run for a third term, Ethel concludes that "I am sure I could not get used to the idea of someone else as President and I do not think Missus Roosevelt could either." Their talks on politics range over the fact that they are lucky to live in Brooklyn because no bombs fall there, that Ethel's Uncle Dan knows there will be another war, and Ethel's Pops's opinion that it is unfair of the government to repossess Carrigan's house. Although he cannot repay his loan, Pops contends that Carrigan has been a loyal citizen in other ways.

The birth of twins adds new material for the column. Joe reports, however, that a fellow whose wife just gave birth to her tenth child was in no mood to congratulate him. Both Ethel and her mother praise Joe when he quits babysitting because he had lasted at least two weeks longer than most men.

All of these columns turn on a small incident, a bit of homespun advice, or an opinion. They add humor and insight regarding ordinary domestic life. As Runyon himself went from boy outcast to man celebrity, the Turps reflect his ability to describe a large subgroup of the American society with which he was never directly affiliated, the working class.

**Short Stories.** While the shorter columns often recall the bedtime conversations of Joe and Ethel Turp regarding their family or neighbors, the dialogue also may involve speculation on politics and world affairs. Joe and Ethel perceive themselves as Little People who are at the mercy of Big People, meaning the law officers and politicians at various levels of government. The two short stories show the Turps scoring limited victories against these larger social forces. When the first of these, "A Call on the President," was made into a movie in 1939, it essentially offered the movie-viewing public a chance to see themselves in a brief moment of triumph. This story is like the Broadway tales in the basic plot structure although the external setting contrasts Little People and Big People instead of the underworld and established society, and the language and tone differ accordingly.

After Jim the mailman is fired because someone saw him burn a letter, Ethel insists that she and Joe go see the President of the United States to have him get Jim's job back despite Joe's objection that "we are only little people and they are big people and what is the use of talking to them?"[18]

Much of the humor is derived from sarcastic exchanges with Washington "cops" who try to dissuade them from calling on the president while they insist that this is one of their rights as citizens of the United States. One policeman finally shows compassion for Joe and tells him where the White House is. When Ethel calls him a hick, instead of being insulted, "the cop ses Buddy I have got one of those too, and I sympathize with you." At the White House when a guard tries to make them leave, a fellow in striped pants intercedes as Joe says, "It is a fine note if a citizen cannot see the President of the United States when he wants to without a lot of cops horning in."

Much of the interest in the interchange between the President and the Turps is drawn from the differing perspectives of this high official and the Brooklynites. As members of the predominant society are referred to by name and the Broadway characters by nickname, in this case the full title is accorded "the President of the United States" whereas the Turps have no claim to distinction. Nonetheless, the president shows a friendly tolerance, and the men meet on near-equal footing. "He ses how are things in Brooklyn? Rotten, I ses. They always are. The Dodgers are doing better but they need more pitching, I ses. How are things in Washington? He ses not so good. He ses I guess we need more pitching here too."

Once the elaborate setting has been established, a rather typical Runyon story unfolds, colored occasionally by the Turps' digressions. Joe relates that Jim the mailman was in love with Kitten O'Brien; and after she married Henry Crusper, Jim "never looked at another broad again. The President of the United States ses another what? Another broad I ses. Another woman I ses. O, he ses. I see." Ethel and Joe exchange a little peripheral domestic chatter that the president seems to enjoy, presumably as a diversion from more weighty matters of state. They finally explain that Henry Crusper died, and Jim the mailman cared for the ailing Missus Crusper and helped raise her son Johnny. Despite Jim's efforts the wild boy had turned into a young gangster. Even though Johnny was able to alienate his mother from Jim, the mailman continued to help them and got Johnny out of trouble as long as that was possible. After Johnny left town, his mother lived on her own dreams of glory for the boy until Jim started writing letters to her in Johnny's name. Then Missus Crusper was able to brag about her son's exploits: ". . . old cromos in the neighborhood whose sons were bums and who had a pretty good idea the letters were phony would set and listen to Missus Crusper read them and tell her Johnny surely was a wonderful man."

The one legitimate letter she received was the one Jim had burned. It was from the warden at San Quentin prison, where Johnny had been a lifer for murder all those years. The letter said Johnny had been killed by the guards as he was trying to escape, and Missus Crusper could have the body if she wanted it.

When the Turps finish this story, the president assures them that he will reinstate Jim the mailman. The matter would have ended with Jim back delivering mail except that Ethel wakes Joe up in the night a couple of weeks later and provides the peripheral twist, again like the Broadway tales. "She ses if ever I go back to Washington again I will give that hick cop a piece of my mind because I have just this minute figured out what he meant when he said he had one of those too and sympathized with you."

The second story about the Turps, "Nothing Happens in Brooklyn," has many similarities with "The Hottest Guy in the World," a Broadway tale published eight years earlier. Both stories revolve around a policeman and a gangster who love the same girl. The policeman wins her largely because he is nearby whereas the gangster is more adventurous as well as being stronger and more competent. The conflict arises when the gangster comes home to see his ailing mother and the girl.

Both Clem Chambers and Big Jule have robbed mail trucks, although Clem's criminality is somewhat downplayed in "Nothing Happens in Brooklyn." Ethel says he is just full of pep, but Joe "ses look Ethel robbing a mail truck is a little different from tying your pig tails to a desk and it is something more than just pep too." Big Jule's long criminal record is also described, including a shooting match in Chicago that "does not count for much as only one party is fatally injured."

In this parody of *King Kong* Big Jule shoots Bongo, an escaped circus gorilla, to save a baby that he had carried to the top of Madison Square Garden. As the baby belongs to Kitty Clancy and Officer Johnny Brannigan, he helps Big Jule escape and visit his

Maw. Likewise, in "Nothing Happens in Brooklyn" the stronger gangster has protected policeman Petey Angelo since childhood because he was the only fellow Myrt McGuire ever had.

When Joe and Ethel Turp hear that the police have Clem Chambers penned up in a building on Clinton Street, Ethel insists that they should go there and tell Clem his Moms is sick. Although Joe "ses Clem may not be seeing callers," Ethel dashes through the police barricade to the building. Petey Angelo is with Clem because he fell through the skylight. Clem bandaged and tied Petey up to protect Myrt's fellow from police gunfire. Ethel convinces Clem that he should give himself up so he can see his Moms. Later, when "they pushed Clem Chambers off at Sing Sing" for shooting a bystander during the gunfight, Ethel tells Joe that Clem had also always loved Myrt McGuire.

While the two short stories and many columns narrated by Joe Turp are somewhat mundane beside the Broadway stories, they are distinctive among Runyon's works in that they reflect an orientation within the mainstream. The law-abiding Turps are part of the working class. As such, they perceive themselves as being at the mercy of larger and more powerful social forces such as law and government. Because they work within the social structure, the Turps come the closest to representing an establishment position of any of Runyon's fictional characters, at least during his later years.

## Chapter Five

# *Tents of Trouble*: Poetry

## Introduction

Casual readers who would normally avoid poetry were more likely to read the verses that Runyon incorporated into his newspaper columns of sports, news, and personal opinion. His poems also occasionally appeared in popular magazines, sandwiched between fiction and articles. Dashed off with more gusto than art, Runyon expected the rhymes to offer a brief chuckle or sentimental pause before even he consigned them to oblivion. Runyon, nonetheless, must have captured a kind of folk humor and wisdom because, while the poems will never win him more than a casual glance and perhaps a shudder from literary critics, often the oblivion was not what Runyon expected. In a sense his poetry is the one sphere in which Runyon pays back a debt to the oral tradition of folk tales from which he borrowed so many anecdotes because his poems have been widely, often anonymously, incorporated in hobo recitation books. They are also familiar around prisons, racetracks, and military installations as part of the oral tradition.

Runyon usually is not given credit for writing what is assumed to be folk poetry with a more distant heritage. Like Thayer's "Casey at the Bat," however, some of Runyon's poems have passed into national folklore. Among those particularly are "Pool Shootin' Roy" and "The Old Horse Player." Others like "Left" and "What the Shell Says" also have been widely and usually anonymously quoted although Runyon's authorship is still generally acknowledged for his most famous poem, "A Handy Guy Like Sande."

Runyon must have recognized that his poems were not likely to enhance his literary reputation because he later claimed that he did not even keep copies of them.[1] What is certain is that he did not list the two earliest books of poetry, *The Tents of Trouble* (1911) and *Rhymes of the Firing Line* (1912), among his collected works in later years. They were again acknowledged, however, when *Poems for Men* was published in 1947. Runyon had begun to edit this volume before his death, and the work was completed by Clark Kinnaird. In much the same format as the two earlier books of verse, a number of poems were republished from them. This demonstrates that Runyon's poetic style remained essentially the same from his earlier years to his last.

Runyon drew graphic portraits that touch a humorous or sentimental vein among readers who like the vernacular and the common touch. Reviewer Leo Kennedy noted his "brilliant and thrifty character drawing" and contended that Runyon's poetic forebears were Robert Service, from whom he learned his favorite ballad forms, and Rudyard Kipling, from whom he learned dramatic lyricism.[2] But the overriding factor is that Runyon's poems were written in much the same popular format that was and still is common in magazines and newspapers. Limericks, rhymed couplets, word puns, and verse vignettes made household words of names like Edgar Guest and Richard Armour as well as Robert Service and numerous colleagues of Runyon's who wrote for the *New York American* and other newspapers. They would readily claim him as one of their own if his reputation had not been further enlarged by the Broadway short fiction.

Runyon offered little to feed the egos of the intellectual elite: no tension or complexity, few symbols or subtleties. His personal mythology is conventional, drawn primarily from universal human emotions. In an infrequent literary allusion, the story of Cain and Abel is retold as an allegory of strikebreaking.[3] Likewise, at one point a hobo attempting to ride the rods while suffering from a hangover compares himself with Chaucer's famous rooster. "I'm roostin' here like a Shantycleer on a rod the size of a match."[4] References to classical mythology are similarly sparse. Steel workers are able to rivet Mars or prop the falling stars "an' make Jove won-

der who's stealin' his lightnin' bolts—." With reference, however
casual, to the Lorelei myth, the Three-Cheers Boys are there when
you win, but they make little noise "When you're stuck somewhere
on the rocks."

Apparently Runyon versified out of some kind of primitive urge,
the songster's joy in creating rhymes, stanzas, and ultimately poems.
They are often rhythmic statements on some of the same topics as
his columns, short vignettes, or simply a deeper human cry for understanding. His verses hark back to the oral tradition of the untutored singer, unlike the erudite scholars who produce much of
today's often highly self-conscious poetry. His poetic form was generally an irregular rhythm created with alliteration and assonance
as well as internal and end rhymes and some sprung rhymes and
rhythms that would make Gerard Manley Hopkins wince.

Sometimes from the point of view of an unidentified narrator,
often in the first person, the speaker usually recalls his reaction to
events as they unfolded. The sequence of thoughts generally leads
to a climax in stanzas interspersed with the repetitions of a refrain.
Runyon often called his poems ballads or songs, and in some ways
they have the simplicity and untutored form of traditional ballads.
The transitions are often abrupt; and the action is frequently developed through dialogue or recollection with little characterization,
depth, or description. Like the ballads of old, tragic situations are
often presented simply; and incremental repetition is common.[5]

In contrast, however, the stanzas are often longer than four lines
and have more than the traditional four/three accented syllable
combinations. In fact, the galloping and often irregular meter suggests that Runyon concentrated on rhyme and let the meter vary
widely according to the speech pattern. In this format, regional
speech and other kinds of dialect are more often duplicated than in
his prose. The dialect, however, was replaced by standard speech
in some of the later poems or those republished in 1947 from the
editions of 1911 and 1912.

Nor do Runyon's poems maintain the impersonal stance toward
the subject that is expected in traditional ballads. Instead, the story
is often revealed through the primary participant's viewpoint and

reaction. Whereas ballads may describe the circumstances of ordinary people rather than the nobility, Runyon took this one step further and wrote about the underdog. Many of his poems express the feelings of the worker, the soldier, or such outcasts from conventional society as the jailbird, hobo, or gambler. Again, "what they do is the best they can," and the protagonists often display a strong streak of deception, even dishonesty, as they attempt to improve their lot and frequently achieve the opposite.

The "Kipling of Colorado" was kidded about such simple refrains as "pants, pants, pants" in a poem about army life; and his lack of taste sometimes combines irregular poetic images that give a sense of embarrassing amateurishness, as when Frisco Red is "churned to a shapeless mass" under the wheels of the fast express. Similarly, some of the galloping lines include parenthetical asides and forced internal and end rhymes that are simply cumbersome, such as "Perhaps he's disappointed and his temper's out of jointed."[6]

That the present tense was no innovation in Runyon's Broadway stories is also evident from some of his earliest uncollected poems such as "Christmus at Jakey's Place" on Larimer Street in Denver, where Ditch Water John, Side Door Pete, and the Cincy Kid enjoy "turk with all the fixins."

> We ask no odds of anyone upon this Christmus day,
>> We envy not th' rich their festive board.
> We hangs our hats in Jakey's place an' sit down
>> Anyway
> An' eats th' best th' market kin afford.
> All on th' Christmus day—
> Sing hey fer Christmus day—
> We hangs our hats in Jakey's place with thanks
>> unto the Lord.[7]

While disasters of language, form, and subject matter are frequent, Runyon occasionally achieved a more successful poetic integration of form and subject matter. In "One o' Langhorne's Men," the wounded doughboy's stream of consciousness imaginatively transports the reader back to his enlistment and wound in the Argonne, as well as through his fantasy of riding away from the hospital as a cavalryman with Lord Langhorne's troops, a reverie broken when a nurse brings him back to reality and the refrain: "Tabbed as a wounded doughboy, an' lookin' a lot the/ part—/ One o' Lord George Langhorne's men an' a cavalry—/ man at heart!"

Runyon's poems are sometimes relatively simple lists, descriptions, or anecdotes. "Reflections of a Gentleman Inside" is essentially a framework on which are woven slang terms for jails such as sneezers, stirs, pokeys, and hoosegows. The slang is considerably more difficult to interpret in verse than in prose where the terms are more readily defined. Runyon translates the French expression *tout de suite,* spelled "toot sweet," as "quick"; but the term "duked" for handshake has to be clarified by the context. The interpretation is complicated because, as in his prose, Runyon sometimes used the same slang word to mean more than one thing. Thus, "from taw" means from the beginning, whereas to have "a taw" means to have a supply of money. Similarly, a "wheezer" is an old person whereas a "wheeze" is an old joke; and these differing meanings are not always clear from the context. Some terms are slang for various nationalities as "Brothers-By-Oath" lists Wops, Spics, and other derogatory ethnic terms represented by sailors in the American navy. They are interspersed with variations on the refrain: "Yesterday, or day before, a member o' th' peerage/ Now he's took a bath an' oath, an' he's American."

Runyon's metaphors are often conventional, such as "the ground slips by like a river," but his verse forms vary widely. For instance, he mixes assonance and feminine rhymes with harsh z sounds to convey a small-town speaker's impression of the Roaring Forties on Broadway. "I'd like to hear the jazzing, and the/ razzing, and the bazzing, the talking/ and the squawking, and the noise of / people walking. . . ." Sometimes the poems revolve around the plays on words such as a refrain by a speaker who asks which horse to bet on, "Which one?" and a bookie who keeps recommending a horse named "Whichone!"

Runyon also frequently used onomatopoeia, as when a bullet tells a soldier, "You ain't agoin back to Al-uh-BAM-ah." The speakers also often hear words in the reverberations from fists, horses' hooves, train whistles, bugles, and other inanimate objects. At reveille a soldier hears the bugle say, "I can't get up" while at taps it says, "Go to sleep." Similarly, an enlisted man in the horse cavalry hears his hunger and disillusionment beaten out in a refrain by the "hoofses" of his mount, "Hunk o' meat an' raw pertater,/ Sop—an' 'tater—sop-an' 'tater!"

### Life Views

In the poems Runyon's speakers often give lip service to ethics and religion; but fear, superstition, and their immediate goals usually enable them to override any moral concerns. Like the first columns in *Short Takes*, "Notes for My Autobiography," several poems in the "After Thoughts" section of *Poems for Men* summarize some of the author's conflicting views. While "They can't rule you off for trying," the father cautions his son about life as well as cards, not to "play 'em unless you've got 'em." Furthermore, Runyon indicates that each man's birthright is the proverbial one good woman and one good dog. If misfortune strikes, however, "Cryin' Won't Git You Nothin'," but loyalty is apt to be rewarded. Runyon's loyalty to his employer William Randolph Heart is reflected in the refrain, "Whose Bread I Eat, His Song I Sing," a viewpoint Runyon also followed as a loyal Hearst reporter for thirty-four years, unlike his recommendation not to gamble, advice he usually ignored.

While the speakers sometimes question the meaning or purpose of some travesty of human life, they most often flounder without an answer. They are usually victims who describe how they try to cope with circumstances beyond their control. The protagonists are limited in education as well as experience and often express their fears, loneliness, and longing, as well as lost love, regret, hate, and superstition. They speak in colloquial or ethnic dialects, often with a minimal or superficial perception of the actual circumstances beyond what they encounter. Whether the soldier tries to summon the courage to die bravely in battle or the athlete copes with underlying fear that he will not be able to measure up, the speakers struggle with the fear of losing their nerve or being down and out. Sometimes a sentimental mood is evoked as they long for the past and their homeland or bemoan the betrayal of love and friendship, often while confronting death. In other cases, these emotions are undercut by a core of realism, often cynicism, in the face of ironic twists of fate, more in the manner of Runyon's short stories. And occasionally the speaker experiences a small triumph, a brief insight, or momentary burst of humor and zest for living.

Religion, superstition, and fear of the unknown surface as ordinary men try to rationalize or cope with exceptional situations or give lip service to traditional beliefs. A man divorcing his longtime wife "cause I'm wantin' 'my whirl' " briefly wonders how he will explain to God. The same is true of the pal who kills a longtime friend who was wounded in battle. While the Deity usually has to wait in line for attention compared with the immediate reality, this priority is elevated, often humorously, when death seems imminent. Thus, an old sergeant invokes his rusty recollections of prayer when he and two others are the badly outnumbered remnants of a scouting detachment in the Spanish-American War. "Now, God, You know I'm no prayist, an' I haven't be-/ spoken You much,/ But it strikes me the time has arriven when we oughta/ get somewhat in touch."

The prospects of death, distance, and declining physical ability invoke a tone of nostalgia under a variety of circumstances. In a poor man's version of Whitman's "Song of Myself," "The Ballad of the Big Town," a speaker who wanders "o' th' Where-You-Wills" all over the world still longs for New York. "But whether I sweat on th' Congo, or freeze on th'/ bergs o' Svork—/ I dream at night o' th' arch o' light that swings over/ Home—New York!" The sentiments of regret and longing also prevail in one of Runyon's few really tender poems, "The Spirit of You": "McSweal of the Battery, speaking—to a locket set/ turquoise blue—/ 'No chaplain to see me departing? Well I'll pray to/ the Spirit of You.' "

This longing for home and the women left behind is common in the military poems. One soldier describes his girl back in Kansas to a "Fat-eyed idol," and another especially longs to hunt nests in the barn with Emmy Marthy Martin. In many instances, however, the lost love has a false and guilty note. As Santa Lee betrays her outlaw lover for gold, often women wait on foreign shores for men who, despite promises to the contrary, never really intended to return.

It is not surprising that some of Runyon's poems were widely published in military newspapers and magazines. He unabashedly praised officers, marines, the Corps of Engineers, and even the rear guard. The uncritical appreciation in these poems starkly contrasts with individual soldiers' more biting reflections on the ongoing dilemmas of war. Both veterans and recruits react to combat and death with bravery, fear, and sometimes cynicism. In one soliloquy an old sergeant ponders his own helplessness while he watches a young recruit's "gills turn blue" as he fights off fear to die bravely, and a sentimental young soldier rallies the broken 19th Horse Cavalry to victory by singing "Nearer My God to Thee" when they are besieged by Del Pilar at Balliug. This contrasts with the less glorious but similarly heroic demise of a scout who says, "Oh, it's us who die in whispers not to give our moves away."

As with his short stories, sorting out the bad from the good and the friends from the enemies often generates some interesting turns of events in the poems. Some of Runyon's most rollicking humor as well as political comment pervades poems about the American army's sometime friends, the Philippinos. Runyon poked vicious fun at the natives who pretended friendship during the day and attacked the Americans at night. The best of these poems is "The Moro Man." He is boisterously described as a peaceful, funny, friendly cuss who lives in a bamboo house and never works or fights. "He likes ter take a shot at us, but jes' for practice'/ sake—." Despite such foibles, the refrain is: "Oh, treat th' Moro gently boys!/ He's Uncle Sammy's Child!" A tone of irony is maintained at the duplicity of the Moro and the foolish benevolence of Uncle Sammy. Nor does the speaker react kindly toward the Americans, who insist on trying to impose their ways on the Moros. "An' you orter hear 'em pray fer you in Uncle Sammy's/ land./ Oh, they'll show you at th' fairs an' they'll double up/ them prayers/ While we chases you with guns, Datto Jan."

Some of these poems gradually unfold as anecdotes with ironic twists that resemble his short stories. At a gravesite in Algeria, a pal mourns his friend who died that day for France. He recalls how "We met as kids in the long ago and we trained to men/ —and crooks." When the girl they both loved chose his pal, they remained friends and went overseas together. But when the pal lay dying, wounded by a "boob-face Arab's knife," he helped death along "wit' the butt o' me gun." Thus, he looks forward to returning to the "frail" back home without fear of retribution because "the dead don't talk, w'ich is nice o' the dead."

### Sports and Other Activities

Convicts, hoboes, athletes, and others who "what they do is the best they can" were often the subjects of Runyon's verse as they were of his columns and short stories. The underdog perspective is apparent as a robber sizes up a jury and concludes that he is unlikely to be freed, while a convict ironically describes "the pleasant family" in Cell House Four. Another notes that all jails are similar in food, conditions, and the prisoners' insistence that they are innocent. Numerous facets of hobo life are also portrayed, such as the problem of clinging to the rods under a train when a hobo has a cinder in his eye or is suffering from a hangover. "Oh, the ground slips by like a river,/ An' me nerves are all a-quiver—/ Fer I've bin out on a sort o' a bat, an' the rail-points/ Sing to me: 'John Barleycorn! John Barleycorn!/ John Barleycorn! John Barleycorn!'"

As in the Broadway tale "Butch Minds the Baby," humor is generated by gangsters trying to conduct business and manage ordinary affairs. Thus, interest and tension are raised by the juxtaposition of apparently discordant elements when a rum runner tries to care for his ailing wife. The "croaker" who recommended a sea voyage to improve Mamie's health surely did not have in mind a rum-running mission between Nassau and Fire Island. To the frequently repeated refrain: "For Mamie's dead in the hold below/ On the cargo o' Black and White!" the narrator recalls such misfortunes of the voyage as an encounter with the revenuers and a gang fight with a mob from Detroit. He also speculates on how he will explain the disappearance "o' them eggs from Harlem" who tried to bury Mamie at sea.

"The Spender" also has a format somewhat like the Broadway stories and injects a note of social comment. The narrator hears the tale from a waiter who bemoans the loss of Daffy Moore's big tips. He earned millions "making junk for the war" and was highly regarded until he stopped spending and started preaching about the stream of blood that flows under the gold. Then his family decided he was "offah his dip" and had him locked away.

Several of Runyon's poems are written from the point of view of professional prize fighters. One waits for the bell to ring and imagines that he hears one of his opponents' gloves say to the other, "Ka-bam! Ka-bam! Ka-bam!" Until then, he had been "Figgahin' to bus' de gemmen's crus' as soon as de gong/ go ding!" Another fighter revises his estimate of how soon he will arrive at a "pahty up in Hahlum" when he realizes that the breeze he feels is from the other fighter's glove passing his chin.

The athletes' nostalgia also can be poignant as age, declining skills, and sometimes penalties force them out of the arenas of glory. Even a great baseball player like Ty Cobb was slowing down by 1925, although he was still better than most players. In "Ol' Ty" his former greatness is recalled with some humor. "But yesterday—how Dad Time jumps—/ I saw him make four smites,/ And steal three bases, slug an umps/ And lick two bleacherites."

A loss of nerve can also end the athlete's career. One baseball player no longer can face left handed pitchers after being knocked out of the batter's box. Similarly, a long-time minor-league player finally recognizes that age and declining skills will prevent him from ever returning to the major leagues. Another ballplayer bemoans the fact that he has been banned from all types of league play because he attempted to get more money. One of Runyon's more successful baseball poems combines the dialogue of a former player taking tickets at a turnstile with his reminiscences of past glories.

When I stepped up in the pinches,
  I'd blow on my bat with my breath,
And you'll find it set down in the record
  How I scart ten pitchers to death!
And no one knew how to run bases,
  And no one could field 'em like me—
"Hey, Mister, this ticket's for Tuesday
  And I never let no one in free!"[8]

Horse racing inspired Runyon's most famous poem, "A Handy Guy Like Sande," which was revised and reprinted several times between 1922 and 1940. The first version celebrated Earl Sande's ability to win. When an injury sustained in a fall from a horse at Saratoga Springs prompted Sande's retirement in 1924, Runyon added a touch of sentimentality that was enhanced fourteen years later when Sande came out of retirement to win the Kentucky Derby. "Say, but I'm young agin', Watchin' that handy/ Guy named Sande,/ Bootin' a winner in!"

The gambler's greed and ultimate debacle are affirmed in Runyon's second most famous poem, "All Hawse Players *Must* Die Broke!" The refrain, "The sucker is a terrible institution!" is a theme that underlies most of the poems about gambling. One bettor wins until "The Fatal Sixth" leaves him broke. Still optimistic, he plans his next day's bets and hopes for better results. Another poem is simply the dialogue of a dice thrower in a crap game as he bets, wins, loses, mourns his loss of luck, and repeats the process. The gambling fever can be so intense that one gambler who is ill immediately begins taking bets on the accuracy of the doctor's prognosis.

In summary, despite their frequently irregular form and awkward rhyme schemes, the substance of these poems maintains a kind of universal appeal because again Runyon speaks as Everyman. He was not a poet but a rhymester whose verses convey some of the hopes, fears, and regrets that his readers readily understand. The selections included in *Poems for Men* are particularly likely to have an optimistic note or cynicism qualified by humor. Those republished from earlier editions are not always the best, but they more accurately reflect Runyon's reputation as a colorful commentator on sports, gambling, war, and the ordinary conditions of life. Notable among these are: loneliness, failure, and disappointment, whether in the big city, military service, or athletics.

## Chapter Six

# The Broadway Stories

## Frame of Reference

In all, Runyon wrote approximately eighty Broadway stories and one play. Most of the stories are included in two collected editions, *The Damon Runyon Omnibus* and *More Guys and Dolls*. Besides the numerous anthologies, movie versions further expanded Runyon's popularity with American audiences. They were especially attracted to the antics of Runyon's racetrack hoods and small-time gangsters during Prohibition when the gap between them and the dominant culture was narrowed by the illegal consumption of alcohol. Runyon's humor continued to divert millions of people during the Great Depression and World War II.

His short stories were popular with the middle-class reader who cherished the rebellion of others but was not brave enough to attempt the same himself. The conservative side was manifested as Runyon also upheld many features of middle-class values such as conformity to proper morals, slang but no vulgarity, and a traditional ending, often the promise of marriage and family. His cynical vein, however, generally suggested that these widely sought goals would not provide the anticipated pleasure, again something his readers knew very well and could also relate to more than the fantasy of living happily ever after. Runyon must have also recognized that violence, including murder, was acceptable and did not need to be justified to his readers under this moral code.

Much of Runyon's humor was developed from the perspective of the outsider, often a small-time hoodlum. The viewpoint that had surfaced occasionally in the early short stories was the lawbreaker's attitude toward the values of the established society. Runyon had begun to play with this theme in early tales about hoboes who used the jails as hotels in "As Between Friends" or took the law into their own hands in "The Informal Execution of Soupbone Pew." This perspective was reinforced by the western code of instant justice or revenge, either of which was likely to be fast and violent.

By the time Runyon's first Broadway story was accepted for publication, he had collected a cast of characters, settings, and plots that reflected twenty years as a newspaperman, primarily in New York but with assignments in Europe and in various parts of the United States. His outlook had broadened, and he had added to his collection of slang and developed a distinctive narrative style through character sketches and vignettes. Runyon had also honed his humor, cynicism, and ability to juxtapose sentimentality, social class, and ethical standards.

The primary aspect of his orientation that Runyon had refined was the relationship between social classes in his fictional community. The interim between early and late short stories reinforced or crystallized his position as an observer who was alien to many socially prescribed values. One significant factor was Runyon's increasing absorption into the sporting and entertainment communities as well as the gangster subculture. The Broadway stories provide a format from which the characters observe, interact with, and sometimes demonstrate moral superiority to the predominant society. While defending the underdog was a frequent theme of the earlier short stories, this cultural contrast is more often mitigated with humor in the later tales.

Certainly Runyon's wide range of acquaintances and acceptance in both the gangster and dominant culture qualified him to play off one element against the other in the Broadway tales. In this effort Runyon's orientation was completely within the immediate community, focused primarily on the difference between appearance and reality rather than good and evil. The overall viewpoint of the short stories conveys insights into distinctly American values of both the dominant and the gangster subculture. Runyon wrote about the world as he perceived it, a society that lived by one set of values while advocating another. The American dream of success through hard work was preached in the schools; but in the streets where Runyon was educated, people lived by another set of standards. Respect was primarily based on wealth regardless of how it was obtained, and this automatically introduced a substantial measure of hypocrisy into the system.

In Runyon's fictional subculture many of the characters do the best they can on the fringes or beyond what is socially acceptable and legal. As money earns respect, how it was obtained is of secondary importance; and inquiring about its origins is not polite or even healthy. In the struggle to turn a dollar, his characters use such means as robbery, gambling, or other illegal activities that could enable them to "chuck a good front" on one occasion and might land them in jail on another.

The hoodlums are rather provincial in that they prefer to associate with their own kind. They distrust outsiders, no doubt partly because of the illegal nature of many of their enterprises that depend on conning members of the dominant society. Most of Runyon's characters are bootleggers, racetrack touts, or ticket hustlers; but others do the best they can in many ways. For instance, the best Pussy McGuire can do is steal expensive cats, whereas Butch's talent is opening safes. Besides their own subgroup, they associate with other frequenters of Broadway who are close enough to be recognized but not integral enough to have nicknames. Among these are Waldo Winchester, the newspaper scribe; Ambrose Hammer, the drama critic; and Johnny Brannigan, the cop. Restaurateurs like Mindy as well as writers, chorus girls, and other regular patrons play only supporting roles unless their individual stories are being told.

Runyon was clearly on the side of the underdogs, among whom he included gamblers and racetrack touts, as well as the purveyors of illegal alcohol by boat and bottle. These underworld characters supposedly maintained a code of loyalty based on individual trust rather than on religion, social position, or compliance with the law. For one thing, the legal system was inequitably applied according to the person's wealth and external badges of status; not that all of the underworld characters were good or consistently adhered to a code of honor by any means. For instance, Runyon's first story introduces Dave the Dude, "who is such a person as would not be shocked at the idea of airing someone, which is a way of saying to kill him." Overall, the Broadway crowd are what their individual characters and circumstances allow them to be, not what the dominant society designates.

Integrity is an individual matter within the subgroup. For instance, The Brain maintains an impeccable reputation for honoring his word although others do not always treat him as well. In contrast, a widow who appears to be poor and righteous earns her living by marrying and then murdering men, a hobby not unknown to other wives in Runyon's stories as well. Small-time touts may hustle outsiders; but gangsters loyally protect the names of those who murder one another from the police, much as legitimate businessmen strive to eliminate competition but refuse to betray industry secrets to outsiders.

Moreover, the illegal bootleggers became legitimate businessmen, importers and brewers of beer, with another Constitutional Amendment that revoked Prohibition in 1933. Thus, Runyon often pointed out that the line between legal and illegal business is fine at best and easily crossed from either side. Whether one is in the banking "dodge" or the bank-robbing "dodge" may mean the difference between knowing the guards and the combination to the safe or having to tunnel in and blast.

Although Runyon biographer Edwin P. Hoyt contended that he was "thumbing his nose at the world of respectability that he mistrusted and despised," Runyon was not indiscriminately on the side of the underworld characters. In matters of honor he was quick to take offense. A gangster who went back on his word or an athlete who tried to throw a game or a boxing match violated the personal code of honor that emphasized loyalty to friends and employers. Most of his stories involve some violation of this code whether by gangsters against one another or by an interaction between social classes, ethnic groups, or men and women.

**Settings**

No matter how much universality is achieved in the writing of fiction, all good prose has at least a national if not a local quality and some reference to a particular era. This reflects at least an unconscious component, a social deposit of information about the particular time and place. In Runyon's case, he became so strongly identified with one place and subculture, the Broadway hoodlums, that social criticism or more universal qualities were often overlooked.

Heywood Broun introduced Runyon's first collected edition of short stories, *Guys and Dolls*, with the observation that every one of them "can be located as having its principal routes somewhere between Times Square and Columbus Circle."[1] Broun found it praiseworthy that Runyon had chosen to write about a single segment of New York, not even all of Broadway. Thus, he concentrated on a more limited area than did the master, O. Henry. This reputation as a local writer of Broadway fiction followed Runyon even though many of the tales take place around the United States or in other countries.

Runyon reinforced the local identification by setting many of the stories in Mindy's. This restaurant became something of a symbol so that in the later stories the characters sometimes express regret that they are unable to partake of Mindy's famous borscht when they are in other locales. Runyon made no secret of the fact that Mindy's was modeled on Leo Lindemann's restaurant, Lindy's, which opened in 1921. Also, Jacob's Beach was named for Libbey's Beach, the sidewalk in front of Lindy's, so dubbed in honor of a racetrack tout who conducted much of his business there.

The year after Lindy's opened, in August 1922, another major piece of the social landscape of the Broadway tales was fitted into place when Runyon made his first trip to Saratoga Springs, New York. He later remembered that everybody from Broadway was there to attend the horse races, so "it felt like standing in front of the Aster Hotel or Reuben's."[2]

In New York, Runyon's characters range freely among various

restaurants and speakeasies such as Good Time Charley's Gingham Shoppe, the more elaborate Crystal Room, or Miss Missouri Martin's Sixteen Hundred Club. In Miami they are likely to frequent Chesty Charles's Sharkskin Grill, but their travels also include Ivy League schools that the ticket scalpers descend upon during various sporting events. In addition, bootleggers hold peace conferences in Atlantic City and conduct their business and other affairs in such secluded spots as small islands off the French Canadian coast or Florida. Enforced vacations under the threat of prison sentences or because of wars also may send the gangsters to various foreign countries including Nicaragua, France, Spain, and North Africa, where they flee or fight in wars.

Despite this variety, probably the Broadway image continued to prevail because, as Nunnally Johnson observed, a Runyon foxhole is almost indistinguishable from Mindy's Restaurant.[3] The appointments are seldom even noted in passing, and the reader is left to fill in his own idea of what the restaurant, speakeasy, or racetrack looks like. This format is successful because the reader is in the company of the narrator. He is clearly familiar with the people and places and usually comments on the quality of the food and liquor, especially the latter. Even Mindy's is known primarily by the cuisine and the clientele, except for the fact that the owner does not appreciate having the patrons accompanied by animals. Because the reader fills in his or her own concept of the setting, Runyon achieves a kind of universality of place that emphasizes the ongoing narrative.

### Point of View

Runyon's short stories were written individually without anything like the master plan of Balzac's *La Comédie Humaine*. The repetition of theme and writing style, however, as well as settings and characters, particularly the narrator, form a kind of community or fictional unit that, taken as a whole, alters the perspective on the individual stories. As in Balzac's novels, Runyon presents a rather large number of characters who appear frequently and provide a material link from one story to another. The major unifying force is the narrator, who conveys a sense of community among the characters with whom he associates and the places he frequents. He achieves a kind of intimacy by telling or listening to a story over a late-night cup of coffee at Mindy's or some other "gaff," which can be a nightclub or, as in this case, a restaurant.

From the first Broadway story in which Runyon's anonymous narrator was introduced, he provides the primary continuity in all of the tales. He is a minor character, a faceless, nameless guy, who is just around. Many of Runyon's friends and family agreed that he was modeled on the author himself. Runyon later was recalled as a quiet, nattily dressed observer who frequented Broadway café society but did far more listening than talking long before cancer of the larynx forced him to communicate by note pad. As Walter Winchell recalled twenty-two years after Runyon's death, "I pass Lindy's where I still seem to see Damon sitting far into the night, silently sipping coffee, listening to the bookies and show girls and gangsters who would later appear in his stories." Runyon's son also drew parallels between his father and the narrator of the Broadway tales as he recalled how Runyon tried to remain a detached observer rather than a participant even in such family matters as the announcement of his son's engagement.

In some Broadway stories the narrator participates and describes the action as it unfolds. In others he is the historian who recounts previous adventures of the gangster subculture. Only in "Ransom . . . $1,000,000" does he have a past and an occupation. The narrator returns to driving a "hack" after the kidnapping and hears about the final turn of events from others.[4] As all of the characters reinforce a group identity of language and viewpoint, the narrative stream switches back and forth from one to another with minimal differentiation.

Runyon's narrative does not alter the perspective by these changes because the characters have a style and group identity stronger than that of the individuals and apart from conventional society. Like Jonathan Swift's satire in which Gulliver's size sometimes is more significant than his individual personality, Runyon's microcosm is also a social stratum to be compared with the dominant society on a collective basis.

Like Gulliver, also, the anonymous narrator establishes the primary focus of events. His biased viewpoint is colored by exaggerations and odd bits of descriptive slang. As the narrator talks or reacts to someone else's telling of a story, his sense impressions are continuously available to the reader. The perspective is usually limited to what he knows by observation, participation, and the accounts of others. As a trusted member of the inner circle, he also can verify their stories for his audience. For instance, he authenticates Dream Street Rose's tale by observing her tar "hoof prints" on Mindy's floor when she leaves. Similarly, after telling how Ida Peters passed up the chance to be a queen to remain true to the memory of Jack O'Donohue, the narrator authenticates the source of the story as Ida Peters herself. She retells it every morning in the restaurant where she serves him coffee.

While the narrator primarily serves as storyteller, he is also an authentic source of information about local events because he is frequently in the company of underworld characters. Despite this, generally the narrator tries to maintain his pose as an innocent bystander. Thus, he accompanies them because he is afraid to decline their invitations in "Blood Pressure," "Dark Delores," and "The Hottest Guy in the World." The police would still call his involvement complicity although he claims to be a timid, law-abiding citizen even when he participates in the recovery of stolen money in "The Three Wise Guys" and as an onlooker in a safe robbery in "Butch Minds the Baby." In some instances, the narrator also controls the turn of events by some kind of action, usually covert.

In "Romance in the Roaring Forties," Runyon's narrator observes the foolishness of columnist Waldo Winchester as he wins Miss Billy Perry away from gangster Dave the Dude, who then wishes to kill him. Instead, the gangster decides to make Miss Billy Perry happy by arranging their wedding. Winchester then is afraid to tell Dave the Dude he is already married because that might cause Dave to follow his original impulse. When Winchester's wife, Lola Sapola, unexpectedly breaks up the wedding, Dave the Dude and

Miss Billy Perry are married instead. Cynicism undercuts the sentiment as the narrator confides that he is the one who called Lola,
and he ponders whether or not he did Dave the Dude a favor at
that.

The narrator's importance in Runyon's short stories was only
gradually recognized by reviewers. Not given much attention in
1931 when *Guys and Dolls* was published, the second collection,
*Blue Plate Special*, motivated a *New York Times* reviewer to describe him as "a likeable fellow, knowing and dumb, brutal and
tender, frank and insinuating."[5] Then in 1938 Fred T. Marsh described the narrator as the most interesting character in *The Best
of Runyon* and "an unforgettable mug in the rogue's gallery of
American fiction." Seen as the prudent guy from around the edges,
the narrator is given credit for being the best historian with a
"pawky" way of telling a story by understatement to make his in-
credible tales sound convincing. "He is a wit, a story teller, an iron-
ist, a wise guy looking to keep out of trouble, a small-timer hanging
on the fringes of big-shot life, tolerated because he's a humorist and
a tower of strength, with his fine baritone in impromptu harmoniz-
ing after the shooting (he always ducks) is over. As he says himself, he's known to one and all as a guy who is just around."[6]

The narrator's status continued to increase until by 1944 Nunnally Johnson was convinced that he was really a money-ball, a
character acceptable to the public, and, thus, "a small gold mine, a
slow, steady, unpretentious oil well." Johnson contended that the
nervous individual who tells Runyon's stories, though handicapped
by existing without any name, "is probably the most resolute Innocent Bystander ever conceived." In this regard, Johnson understated
the narrator's actual level of participation but not his importance.

## Character Development

Generally, the best short fiction has plots that emerge out of the
characters to portray the author's personal world in universal terms.
A good character is expected to be both an individual and a type.
Thus, conflicting traits, emotions, and behavior patterns convey

unique as well as common qualities in each person. Many conflicts involve the clash of diverse characteristics in an individual such as tough and tender, positive and negative.

Runyon's stereotyped characters seldom gave individual expression to his overall point of view although he also repeatedly emphasized the importance of character over plot. Gene Fowler recalled him saying: "And to hell with plots, because nobody ever remembers much about the plots of Dickens or Mark Twain. They remember the characters."[7] Runyon never attempted the sustained character and plot development of a novel. Perhaps, like Poe, he recognized that his talent was best restricted to describing shorter periods of sustained action. Instead, Runyon limited his revelations of individual characters and emphasized their interactions with one another and the dominant society.

As Runyon's fiction became more popular, it was a matter of local pride to claim that his characters originated in Denver as well as in New York. Probably this also reflected his reputation as a humorist rather than a social satirist. Denverites contend that Runyon drew materials from frequenting Matty Silks's bordello and other establishments on Larimer Street. They later claimed that the models for such characters as Nicely-Nicely Jones, Nathan Detroit, and Sky Masterson were taken from this earlier period.

Since Runyon spent a maximum of five years as a working newspaperman in Denver, primarily between 1906 and 1910, the balance of the argument tends to favor the New York side because he spent almost twenty years in the Big City before the Broadway short stories were published. Then Heywood Broun's introduction to *Guys and Dolls* established a claim of authority and authenticity for the way Runyon portrayed the Broadway characters. He praised how Runyon "caught with a high degree of insight the actual tone and phrase of gangsters and racketeers of this town. Their talk is put down almost literally." Heywood Broun contended that he recognized the various characters as actual people "who are at this moment living and loving, fighting and scuttling no more than a quarter of a mile from the place in which I live."

Indeed, some characters are thinly veiled fictionalizations of living people. For instance, in his first Broadway story, "Romance in the Roaring Forties," Runyon introduced a newscaster named Waldo Winchester who resembles the well-known columnist Walter Winchell. When this story was collected along with the others in *Guys and Dolls*, a *New York Times* critic noted that the action of the stories was aided by the authentic manner in which Runyon reproduced the language of his Broadway—words, phrases, tones, and isms. This reviewer also suggested that the reader might enjoy speculating on the possible identity of such characters as Miss Missouri Martin, the operator of the Sixteen Hundred Club, as well as The Brain and Big Butch the safecracker.[8]

Similarly, Winchell praised Runyon's authenticity in his introduction to *Blue Plate Special*. He noted Runyon's wide range of acquaintances from Johnny Broderick, a detective at Madison Square Garden and presumably the prototype for Officer Johnny Brannigan, to such better-known figures as gangster Al Capone and Mayor Jimmy Walker. Winchell proclaimed that *Blue Plate Special* furthered Runyon's reputation as an outstanding reporter as well as "the most exciting and spellbinding of historians and an expert on crime." Winchell contended that outlaws on both coasts respected his opinions on sports and also his articles on crime. "The lethal sock he packs in his pillars of pithy patter for the paper—has driven mobsters out of New York faster than an extra girl in Hollywood says 'Yes.' "[9]

Presumably Runyon's fictional gangsters were based on the ones he knew in real life. In fact, according to Winchell, in some instances they derived status from their fictional representation. This is somewhat ironic because of the secretive nature of their unlawful occupations. But not all gangsters shrank from publicity as long as it was not focused on their illegal activities. As Winchell recalled later, "One night a regular customer rushed into Lindy's and excitedly announced, 'Hey—in the new Runyon story—the character who kills three guys! It's me. Just think. Me!' "[10]

Despite being based on real people in some cases, Runyon's characters have very limited descriptions or development in the short stories. Colorful nicknames or "monikers" often identify members of the Broadway subculture by appearance, background, or occupation, such as Blondy Swanson, Nathan Detroit, and Regret the Horse Player. Except for these nicknames, they are likely to be described only in terms of matters that relate directly to the development of the plot.

As with the *In Our Town* character sketches, many of the titles of the Broadway stories identify the major characters. These include Little Miss Marker, the Lemon Drop Kid, and Madame La Gimp. Others reflect central events, such as "Butch Minds the Baby" or the twist in the cases of "Blood Pressure" and "Pick the Winner." Sometimes the titles seem overly cute and contrived. For instance, in "Too Much Pep" hit man Don Pep scares Ignaz the Wolf to death.

The names also indicate the relationships among individuals and groups of people. Generally, nicknames were reserved for members of the subgroup with whom the narrator of the stories identified. Outsiders are called by their legal names or "square monikers"; and they are often accorded full, formal titles such as Mr. Paul D. Veere. On the other hand, Frankie Ferocious, Joey Perhaps, and Don Pep are not otherwise identified.

These characters generate a new perspective and often humor when identified in the frame of reference of the established society. For instance, Butch the safecracker has a son named John Ignatius Junior; and the child named after Blondy Swanson is called Olaf. Women particularly indicate their role as outsiders by referring to the characters by their "square monikers." Miss Hilda Slocum knows Nicely-Nicely Jones as Quentin, and Miss Clarice Van Cleve refers to Gigolo Georgie as Elliot. Women also are accorded the titles of Miss or Mrs., as men from the dominant society are often called Mr., frequently as a dubious gesture of respect.

Many names have ironic overtones, and some have multiple meanings. The timid Tobias Tweeney is ironically tagged "Tobias the Terrible" to conform with his new but false reputation as a tough gangster. Sky Masterson has a "sky's the limit" image as a gambler, knows the Bible from reading it in hotel rooms, and falls in love with a missionary worker named Sarah Brown. Appropriately, when he marries her and becomes a drummer in the mission band, Sky is called by his given name, the biblical Obediah.

In most cases, the names the subculture assigns to the characters are more appropriate than the idealistic given names attached by fond parents. Some of them also can be quite cruel, such as Dumb Dan the Indian, a character in one of the stories of my old hometown out West. Proper names may also convey overtones, as drama critic Ambrose Hammer not only hammers but, in fact, "harpoons" actors with his critiques of their performances. The Joe and Ethel Turp stories, however, are about working-class society, and the characters are usually called by their given names. The same is true for many individuals in my old hometown out West.

While the nicknames may be interpreted as a form of condescension, they can also signal acceptance, as does appropriate "in group" slang in various subcultures. Thus, both are also common among American teenagers, who seek a strong peer-group identity apart from the dominant adult society. Pseudonyms are also common among writers and newspaper columnists. While Runyon's by-line also accompanied columns authored under the names of A. Mugg, Joe Turp, or other characters he created, in the same era sports news was reported under the by-line "A. Baseball," and financial information ostensibly came from the pen of "Broaden Wall." Thus, from the elementary schoolyard through the hobo camps and newspaper offices to the subculture of the gangsters, the use of nicknames was common. Like the citizens' band radio "handles" of today, Runyon's titles often also invoke alliteration and/or assonance so that a poetic rhythm is added by their constant repetition as, more often than not, Runyon repeats the entire name. Regret the Horse Player may sometimes be called Regret, but Hot Horse Herbie is never just Hot. The trio Harry the Horse, Spanish John, and Little Isadore are all listed when they are mentioned together just as Runyon repeats the phrase "my old hometown out West" until it is almost a slogan long after the setting has been well established. This repetition of names, like the use of fixed expressions, lent an artificial quality so that even authentic responses by the characters were less likely to be recognized and accepted as such.

## Chapter Seven

# Humor

## Frame of Reference

E. M. Forster contended that a plot can be defined as a narrative of events with the emphasis on causality.[1] Plots can be developed satisfactorily either with tight causal relationships or a fair degree of vagueness, but bad plots falsify life. Runyon was criticized for plots that rely too much on coincidence and an overly structured ordering of time, place, and events. Runyon's overall rather simplistic writing formula was: "Make 'em laugh and make 'em cry."[2] To accomplish this, the stories often were composed of four basic ingredients: love, larceny, violence, and some kind of twist often based on coincidence.

Runyon combined a vivid narrative style and boisterous humor that forced the reader into a new perspective on his or her own society and the hoodlum subculture. But the primary purpose was to entertain; and Runyon's short stories often include some kind of social satire, parodies of common literary themes or stories, and even the retelling of old jokes.

To emphasize humor and social comment, Runyon forfeited his exceptional talent for description. His forte in newspaper writing was an eye for detail. The way he represented the mannerisms of baseball players and boxers turned them into box-office attractions, but his short stories turn on stereotyped characters in generalized settings.

The basic structure of Runyon's short stories depends on the single, detached episode common to all anecdotes, jokes, and yarns. They extended his columns, which were sometimes anecdotes illustrating a moral point or a celebrity's character.[3] In other cases, they were miscellaneous collections of information and opinion. The short stories are more like the vignettes with organized plots that were published as Sunday features. These yarns turn on a single incident whereas the short stories sometimes have more detailed and complicated plots, but all were designed as humorous comments on society.

The questions of what constitutes humor and its social impact have been widely debated. Henri Bergson contends that nothing is comic apart from human beings.[4] Thus, apes are humorous only insofar as their actions appear to imitate people. By the same token, laughter is generated when a person gives the impression of being a thing. Human beings who imitate robots are amusing, just as the concept of disguise has a comic quality. Calling a Negro unwashed, soot, or Runyon's term, "stovelid," demonstrates a logic of imagination rather than reason, a kind of humor despite the racial slur.

Comedy represents a callousness toward social life that arises from a mechanical inelasticity of mind. It can result from absent-mindedness, preoccupation with the past, or rigidity of professional behavior or language. In any of these circumstances, the individual acts automatically in a routinized and artificial manner. Any person is comic when he automatically goes his own way without troubling himself about getting in touch with the rest of his fellow beings.[5] Humor can be generated by any substitution of artificial for natural, of something mechanical encrusted upon the life processes that seems to usurp the laws of nature. Thus, humor is often derived because what happens seems to be out of sequence or is not sensible in the context.

Professional behavior becomes humorous when it is so routine as to seem mechanical, and the same is true of professional language. This effect can also be achieved by members of trades and public services. Runyon gave the gangsters this mechanical quality by their innocent manner of going about their normal business so their actions seem rigid to outsiders. Their distinctive terminology also makes them colorful. The hoodlums seem humorous in themselves and in comparison with the rigid behavior in authentic professions with which Runyon sometimes drew parallels.

Professional logic can also be humorous. The customary reasoning processes in one occupation appear valid for the participants but may look ridiculous to outsiders. Thus, the jargon of medicine or law can sound like gobbledygook to laymen. Because the responses to individual situations seem mechanical rather than authentic, this quality can easily transform common sense into comic absurdity, the comic logic that Bergson contends is of the same nature as dreams. Thus, laughter is provoked by what is false in real life, but the same thing might be accepted as true in a dream. This kind of logic is relaxing because it lacks tension and affords relief from intellectual effort. Like Coleridge's willing suspension of disbelief, this willingness to play based on intellectual distance enabled Runyon's readers to find humor even in such brutality as gang killings.

Light comedy can be an artificial exaggeration or a natural rigidity in handling life situations. Actions and relations seem to give life a mechanical quality as they are repeated or transferred to another set of actions and relations with which they partially coincide. Runyon exercised a common method of provoking laughter. He transferred old ideas into fresh surroundings, transposing them into a different key and style so the new version gains humor by comparison with the old. Like everyone else, the gangsters play practical jokes and struggle with domestic problems but within the context of their more sinister business. They demonstrate a ritualistic quality because the behavior seems unnatural from the point of view of what is expected within conventional social conditioning. The biblical teaching "Do unto Others as You Would Have Others Do unto You" is given a cynical reversal in Runyon's stories. Sometimes the perspective is startling and humorous because the characters respond to natural instincts such as the desire for vengeance instead of turning the other cheek.

Readers were entertained by the violent behavior of Runyon's hoodlums and other characters because of their distance from emotional involvement. Comedy is an intellectual experience that depends not on right and wrong but on manners or ideas, the prejudices of a society. The faults of others create laughter because of their unsociability rather than their immorality. Thus, even a vice can be ludicrous, and either serious or trifling matters can generate laughter if the reader's emotions are not aroused. Runyon threw a wet blanket on sympathy for his characters by undercutting this reaction with cynicism. Although Max Eastman contends that humor can be close to pathos, the laughter is strained when sympathy for Runyon's characters is not adequately counteracted.[6] For example, in "Johnny One Eye" a child's one-eyed cat is sacrificed to give a gangster a well-placed shot at his adversary. His dying recommendation that the child be given a new cat with two good eyes and the promise of a reward are not sufficient to overcome the somber tone generated by the preceding violence.[7]

All humor involves some social satire because it is created through rituals of human behavior regarding character, circumstances, and/or language. Satire includes irony, which states what ought to be done and pretends that it is actually being done. In contrast, satire also encompasses humor, which describes what is actually being done under the pretense that this is what ought to be. Thus, humor is the counterpart of irony. "Both are forms of satire, but irony is oratorical in its nature, whilst humor partakes of the scientific." Humor can transpose ideas from moral to scientific. By the same token, ideas of everyday life can be transposed into professional jargon, or business phraseology can be transposed into the social relations of life. Either reversal is comic. Therefore, Bergson contends that, in a sense, "a humorist is a moralist disguised as a scientist."[8]

Runyon transposed the society and business of gangsters with those of their respectable counterparts to satirize both. By juxtaposing the social classes, he tried to break down the readers' illusions about good and evil. Runyon drew attention to the artificial quality of what Herman Melville called "that manufacturable thing known as respectability," for which moral value is the raw material.[9] Jean Wagner contended that Runyon fired shots at the legitimate society while drawing the readers' attention away from his target with his "no-account guys and dolls." Critics took exception to Runyon's distortions because they assumed that his underworld was presented for its own sake rather than as a satire on the dominant society. "In fact, however, the writer's primary concern is with the legitimate world, and Gangland is really nothing more than his Lilliput or his Brobdingnag,—a convenient yardstick with the help of which he can measure the lag between society's ideal values and its actual ones."

Drawing a parallel with Jonathan Swift's *Gulliver's Travels*, Wagner contended that attention was primarily focused on Runyon's gangsters because they hold so much fascination for the legitimate society that the juxtaposition of one group against the other was usually overlooked. This was like seeing Swift's Houyhnhnms and overlooking the Yahoos. On this basis the critics resemble an Irish bishop whom Swift recalled as saying that *Gulliver's Travels* was "full of improbable lies, and for his part he hardly believed a word of it."[10]

Runyon's satire differs from Swift's, however, in that Runyon's scale constantly changes as gangland and the larger American social structure are satirized in terms of each other.

With Runyon, the problem is slightly more complicated. His scale undergoes constant variations even as the story proceeds. In fact, every element in this fiction is a variable in its own right, because he does not compare real human beings with imaginary ones, but with other real human beings,—an actual social category with another, each of them with its own qualities and defects, but also with a number of prejudices in terms of which it views and evaluates the category against which it is pitted.[11]

Runyon was charged with falsifying life in comparison with serious writers of short fiction. Unlike them, however, his goal was to produce humorous satire; and the nature of comedy is to portray general types already familiar to the reader instead of individuals. Comedy has been defined as standing midway between art and life because it strives for generality whereas art aims to create the individual. Thus, comedy is directed outward at the point where persons become capable of resembling others. The observation is external and the result is general, expressing average mankind as comedy brings together scattered data, comparing analogous cases and extracting their essence by abstraction and generalization.

To achieve humor, characters can be generalized even to the extent of creating satellites with the same basic traits as the main character. Then the humor of self-repetition is added by reinforcement with different copies of the same model. Certainly Runyon takes advantage of this humorous tactic, as all of his hoodlums resemble one another. They all talk like the narrator and often have the same response of innocence and naiveté in relation to the dominant society. Their artificiality demonstrates Bergson's contention that "whether a character is good or bad is of little moment: granted he is unsociable, he is capable of being comic."[12]

Comic characters, then, are types that demonstrate how one can unconsciously fall out of authentic behavior and into a ready-made category. The comic character may demonstrate such qualities as rigidity, automatism, absentmindedness, or unsociability. An individual's professional isolation can be of such a high degree that he becomes like an automaton. As the comic person has an unconscious rigidity, his comic feature is in proportion to his being ignorant of himself, unaware of this quality. Runyon's characters are immersed in themselves as they conduct their business in contrast with the dominant society. They reflect Max Eastman's definition of a comic person as "someone who is somehow 'off,' or 'out of true,' and yet possesses the magnetism necessary to attract you to this." Because they act automatically without making individual responses to their environment, the humor depends primarily on interchanges between the characters without regard for a particular setting or time.

Comic types are impertinent toward the audience who laugh first because of identification with or sympathy for them. The comic character is regarded as a playmate, and the immediate response of laughter produces relaxation. Comic absurdity gives the impression of playing with ideas, but laughter also has a larger social function. It is primarily a corrective intended to repress the separatist tendencies that distinguish the comic character from others in the society, converting rigidity into plasticity. Laughter has always reflected an unconscious desire to humiliate and correct another, in deed if not in will. To accomplish this, a painful impression is made on the person toward whom it is directed.[13] This punishes some feelings in everyone, striking the innocent as well as the guilty, because laughter aims at a general result, not the individual case. Runyon's gangsters are laughable first because they demonstrate ordinary human characteristics within the framework of an unusual setting. Second, their deviation from accepted behavior gives the reader an opportunity to laugh and diffuse fear or objections to their unsocial behavior. In a sense, then, laughter can be interpreted as a social gesture that restrains eccentricity with the aim of general improvement.

The audience relates to the mischief-makers on one level as the rebels they would also like to be and then turns to laughter as "a spark of spitefulness or at least mischief" with the intended goal of social betterment. According to Bergson, laughter indicates a slight revolt on the surface of social life. "It instantly adopts the changing forms of the disturbance. It is gaity itself. But the philosopher who gathers a handful to taste may find that the substance is scanty, and the after taste bitter."[14] Literary critics who compared Runyon with serious authors of short fiction indeed found the substance scanty. For this his work was berated and his humor downplayed, although it warranted comparison with that of Ring Lardner, James Thurber, and Dorothy Parker. Even lines like "Men seldom make passes/ At girls who wear glasses" assumed an aura of sophistication in the pages of the *New Yorker*. But Runyon's humor appeared in newspapers and magazines of more general circulation where the gangster perspective also drew attention away from humor that satirized more universal human behavior.

## Social Satire

**Gangster Activities.** While some of Runyon's short stories maintain a consistently humorous tone, others descend into sentiment or pathos. The gangster stories all have essentially the same general plot structure, however. In each episode Runyon's hoodlums must extricate themselves from some kind of predicament, often involving members of the established society. Sometimes the good deed is central to the plot, and other times it is peripheral, as with the twist at the end. The more natural and spontaneous the action, generally the more successful the story, whether the overall tone is humorous or not.

The best of Runyon's humor resembles Bergson's definition of comedy as a game that imitates life: "The more natural the cause, the more comic the effect."[15] Jokes are acceptable if they seem to be the natural product of a particular state of mind or in keeping with the circumstances. The arrangement of events is comic if the single combination has the illusion of life and the distinct impression of a mechanical arrangement. Unlike light comedy and farce, which are in contrast with reality, the higher comedy rises, the more it approximates life. By the same token, freedom is serious, but its appearance is comic. Therefore, the master is serious, but the servant imitating him is humorous. A party in the larger society is simply a party; but when Runyon's gangsters imitate this behavior, the result is humorous; and a party that mixes the two social groups can be a comic disaster.

Some of Runyon's most effective humor transposes the ordinary activities of regular citizens into the gangster context so that two independent series of actions are juxtaposed against one another. One distinctive example of this is "Butch Minds the Baby." Butch is prevailed upon by Harry the Horse, Little Isadore, and Spanish John to open a safe. Because he has to babysit with son John Ignatius Junior, Butch insists that the baby be cut in for 5 percent to "round himself up with his ever-loving wife in case of a beef from her over keeping the baby out in the night air."[16] From then on the plot revolves around trying to keep the baby quiet while they open the safe. The hoodlums warm the bottle and let the baby chew on a stick of dynamite. Finally, they get away safely because the police do not suspect that anyone would take a baby along on a robbery.

As ordinary activities seem unnatural within the gangster context, these stories demonstrate that comedy often results when a situation belongs simultaneously to two independent series of events. The coincidence of the two must be kept before the audience to enable them to laugh at the reciprocals. This parallel is more consistently maintained in "Butch Minds the Baby" than in most of Runyon's other stories.

This simultaneous structure is also demonstrated in one of Runyon's most famous short stories, "Madame La Gimp." The gangsters satirize respectable society by holding up a mirror, albeit a distorted carnival mirror, that invokes laughter as well as insight into social pretensions. Influential citizens are impersonated at Dave the Dude's reception for Madame La Gimp. Her daughter is in town to introduce her fiancé and his parents, Spanish noblemen. The pretension is necessary because the daughter does not know that her mother is a charwoman, having been away at school for many years. Much of the humor is derived from gangsters who assume various roles. The "police commissioner" is wanted by the law in several states, and Nick the Greek is insulted that he is asked to impersonate Heywood Broun. After the foreign guests leave town, Dave the Dude asks the others to return all of the stolen goods, including the grand piano.

"Madame La Gimp" follows the plot formula in many of Runyon's stories after "Romance in the Roaring Forties" introduced the contrast between the established society and the hoodlums concerning love and a related deception. The romance surrounding gangsters during Prohibition made this attraction and deception seem more feasible. In this first story Waldo Winchester says people like to read about gangsters because they seem romantic. Likewise, in "Social Error" Winchester explains that newspapers make heroes out of gangsters so that people with an underworld complex want to associate with the tough guys.

Runyon satirized this foible of the dominant culture in "Social Error" and "Tobias the Terrible." In the first story Miss Harriet Mackyle asks Dave the Dude to bring some tough guys to her party. Waldo Winchester says they add color, and Dave the Dude agrees to comply with the request because he is a bootlegger and Mackyle is a good customer. The humor is generated because the gangsters seem naive and out of place as they attempt to socialize.

The same attraction to the gangster culture is reflected in "Tobias the Terrible." Since Deborah Weems dates Joe Trivett and he boot-legs ginger extract, Tobias Tweeney also wants to impress her with how tough he is. At Good Time Charley's Little Gingham Shoppe, all of the gangsters sympathetically discuss how Tobias might meet some gangsters. Then the police raid, and they hide their guns on him. In court Tobias tips over from the weight and ironically earns the nickname "Tobias the Terrible" when the guns are exposed.

**Love and Marriage.** In Runyon's fictional society, the big adventure of life is to find love while most of the smaller adventures revolve around attempts to find the other important commodity, money. The second is the key to the first as well as to everything else. Status, love, and security all revolve around money. When they have it, the gangsters usually lavish such tokens as jewels and furs on chorus girls who see their route to social prominence primarily as marriage to a rich man. Thus, the hood is likely to be put aside even if his love is truer than that of a respectable suitor with status and presumably wealth.

Runyon's contempt for wealthy patrons who "slummed" among his people along Broadway was well defined by 1921. In one of his columns he quoted a long section of *American Notes* in which Charles Dickens described the pigs along Broadway eighty years be-fore. In Dickens's time, the ladies had to pick their way carefully as the pigs lumbered freely along searching for garbage, watchful only for their old enemies, the dogs. Runyon contended that Broad-way still had its share of pigs, "only they have taken on the sem-blance of humans. . . . Of an evening they gather in cabarets, wallowing in illicit liquor, and snouting through a conversational garbage made up of oaths and filthy stories and scandal. A pig is a pig, even when it wears evening clothes. The pigs that roamed Broadway eighty years ago had at least the merit of not trying to disguise their breed."[17]

Although Runyon hobnobbed with the rich and famous while he

gambled and frequented the "hot spots," his fiction reflected a high degree of hostility toward the established citizens, especially the wealthy and prestigious upper classes, who either inherited or appropriated their money by legal means. They were able to maintain their status or at least "chuck a good front," giving the appearance of wealth and power as they came to Broadway to gamble, drink, and seduce the chorus girls. This was the theme of several stories. For example, in "The Bloodhounds of Broadway" Lovey Lou, a dancer at Miss Missouri Martin's nightclub, shoots Marvin Clay "smack dab in the chest" for what he did to her and her sister. This crime is solved despite the fact that John Wangle's bloodhounds track Big Nig, who has been feeding them, instead of following the killer.

Runyon demonstrates that status and respectability depend on wealth instead of integrity because prominent citizens often have backgrounds that are similar to those of his hoodlums. Despite the class differences, then, the claim to moral and legal respectability frequently depends on who pays for the dirty work and who carries it out. That wealth and then social polish are the only prerequisites for social standing is demonstrated in "Ransom . . . $1,000,000," "Neat Strip," and Runyon's play *A Slight Case of Murder*.

In "Ransom . . . $1,000,000" John Withington White III is kidnapped by Dan the Devil, and he falls in love with Dan's daughter Francesca. She is afraid the daughter of a gangster would not be accepted in his society, but John Withington White III assures her that one of his ancestors was hanged for piracy and another was chased out of San Francisco by the vigilantes for swindling the Forty-Niners. Therefore, "If you can stand for my family, I can stand for yours."

Unlike these social class differences, the theme of love and its betrayal was common to both hoodlums and "swells." As Hawthorne chose adultery as a sin of human weakness in *The Scarlet Letter*, readers could relate to seeking and betraying love in all social circumstances. Max Eastman, however, contends that "all vigorously imaginative humorists exaggerate," and Runyon sometimes stretched his plots to achieve comic absurdity.

True and unrequited love is demonstrated among the upper crust in "The Old Doll's House." While Abigail Ardsley "has practically all the potatoes in the world, except maybe a few left over for general circulation," she keeps her clocks set at twelve o'clock for forty-five years in remembrance of the last time she saw her lover alive. Bootlegger Lance McGowan uses this fact to alibi the time when he shot rival bootleggers: Angie the Ox, Mockie Max, and the Louse Kid.

At the other end of the social scale, a busboy named Little Pinks is of too low status to win the hand of a dancer named Your Highness even after she is crippled. Nonetheless, Little Pinks pushes her wheelchair to Florida in the winter, and even steals jewelry for her because she thinks it will attract men. After she dies, he violates his parole to break the spine of the man who crippled her.

Sometimes Runyon simply retold popular stories in the language and social context of his Broadway hoodlums. One, "The Three Wise Guys," turns the Christmas story into a gangster odyssey. The narrator joins Blondy Swanson and the Dutchman on Christmas Eve as they set out to retrieve money stolen in a factory holdup. The trio follows a star to a barn where Clarabelle Cobb is giving birth. Her husband, Joseph, has been falsely accused of complicity in the robbery, so they leave the gripsack full of money to free him. On their return trip, the trio is stopped for speeding in Bethlehem, Pennsylvania; but the policeman does not ticket them because it is Christmas. They, in turn, give thanks that they did not have the stolen money in their possession.

**Competition: Sports and War.**    Members of the dominant culture are often deceived by small-time hoodlums in stories about college athletics, boxing, horse racing, and baseball. Sometimes the impostors are revealed and rejected. In other cases, the circumstances are righted by assimilating individuals from one group into the other.

College athletic events emphasize the class conflict in two stories about Sam the Gonoph's team of ticket scalpers. They unmask one of their own who impersonates a legitimate citizen in "A Nice Price." A wealthy Yale man gratefully covers his betting losses after a rowing meet because Sam prevents Society Max from marrying his sister. Society Max had stolen Sam's fiancée previously, so Sam chases him off the Yale man's yacht. Then the Harvards win because a Yale oarsman hits Max's head with an oar.

Three stories about boxing—"Bred for Battle," "The Big Umbrella," and "Leopard's Spots"—all center on the efforts of fight promoter Spider McCoy to develop a winning heavyweight boxer, much as Runyon tried to own a piece of a winning fighter; but he also succeeded only in supporting a group of losers. Blood lines are one way Spider McCoy tries to select a prospective fighter, although being of royal descent does not help. Spider's niece, Margie Grogan, contends that a former king named Jonas is just another big umbrella, a prize fighter who folds up as soon as someone hits him. After Jonas is recalled to assume the throne, however, Margie marries him, and Spider McCoy marries the sister of dictator Polta Fuss. Nor is the model of breeding animals with good blood lines altogether successful. In "Bred for Battle" Spider McCoy is disappointed that the first-born son of Shamus Mulrooney and Briget O'Shea is delicate and likes to play the zither, as did a clerk with whom O'Shea was friendly before she married Mulrooney. McCoy is consoled, however, when he meets the second son, Terence. He is a lightweight but a fighter like his father.

Runyon's longest short story, "Money From Home," and several others deal with various aspects of horse racing from placing bets to the horses' retirement. While naturalism is not a conscious feature of Runyon's fiction, events often turn on luck or coincidence. Fate prevails instead of planning as fortune and romance often ride with bets on horses. Although the races are frequently rigged, the odds fall toward losing as Runyon reinforces his old slogan that all horse players must die broke.

In "A Story Goes With It," a man named Harter decides not to commit suicide after he wins by betting on a horse named Never Despair. The race was fixed because the jockeys wanted the horse's owner to be able to pay for his crippled daughter's surgery. Nonetheless, the narrator loses because he ignored Hot Horse Herbie's tip and bet on a horse by the name of Loose Living.

Frequently, Runyon's satires involve a twist on true love and some other topic. For example, the southern-belle tradition is satirized in "It Comes Up Mud" when Miss Beulah Beauregard breaks her engagement to a banker and returns to her father's farm in Georgia. Unlike the women of grace and leisure in the grand antebellum plantation tradition, she is plowing with a mule when Little Alphie finds her. He then earns as much money as he would by winning the Kentucky Derby by loaning a horse named Last Hope to the banker. He needs to hurry to catch a train back to New York and avoid prosecution for embezzlement.

When social revolution is given a Broadway twist, the conflict is between rich and poor instead of gangster and respectable citizen, more in the manner of the two short stories about the Turps. In "Tight Shoes," after a hard-working shoe salesman, Rupert Salsinger, is fired, he goes on a drinking spree with wealthy young Calvin Colby, and they join the crowd in Columbus Circle. When Salsinger speaks out against the rich, Colby is bored and starts a march. Others follow and demolish the shoe store. The unlikely pair are publicized as organizers for social justice; and Colby's parents support the movement because they think it is more useful than spilling "dolls" out of cars, Colby's usual occupation. While Salsinger is running for Congress, Colby looks after his girl friend, Minnie Schults. When Rupert decides to propose, his shoes hurt and he misses the appointment. By the time he arrives, Minnie Schults has accepted Colby's proposal.

Some stories concern the war effort although Runyon was too old to be anything but a distant observer in World War II. He satirizes drama critics in "The Melancholy Dane." After a tour of duty in North Africa as a war correspondent, Ambrose Hammer describes how an actor named Mansfield Sothern forced him to listen to a repetition of Hamlet's graveyard scene before he would carry the wounded drama critic safely through the German lines. Later, Hammer takes the narrator to see Sothern play Hamlet. The egotistical actor is still not satisfied with a great review, the assurance of Chanelle Cooper's love, and high praise from Professor Bierbauer. As a German officer, he had overheard Sothern's performance when they were surrounded.

Runyon's most joyous war story, "Big Boy Blues," recounts the reactions of a tough hoodlum who learns that his son is impersonating a female ballet dancer in a soldiers' musical comedy called *Gee Eyes* rather than fighting in the South Pacific. In this satire on the macho fighting man, the father is proud of his son instead of being angry; but the ticket scalper who told the narrator about Little Boy's act winds up in the Pacific theater with Coogan's Cobras.

Despite a somewhat mechanical plot structure reinforced by the twist at the end, the basis of Runyon's humor in various kinds of satire is clearly evident. The humorous perspective is further enhanced by his descriptions of individual reactions to the circumstances. While the satire of one group by another is not consistent, the circumstances often are highly predictable. This feature also has a comic quality, particularly as it is reinforced by Runyon's linguistic style—the slang, set expressions, and predominant present tense that were his trademarks.

## Chapter Eight

# Runyonese

## Background, Present Tense

As Mark Twain's influence can be demonstrated in the my-old-hometown-out-West plots and humor, Bret Harte's impact on Runyon's writing style was evident in the later as well as the earlier fiction. Runyon recalled Harte's description of Jack Hamlin, the famous gambler, "with his pale Greek face, and Homeric gravity" in describing Arnold Rothstein and Nick the Greek.[1] Moreover, just as the plots of Harte's "The Luck of Roaring Camp" and Runyon's "Little Miss Marker" are very similar, the two writers also exhibit other parallels in their fictional formula.

Both men used a grim, sordid background which was romanticized almost beyond recognition, and they played this setting alternately for superficial laughs and sentimental tears. Both used a set of rootless and unprincipled characters who could easily be made astonishing because they did not have to be made credible. Both used a style employing rather specious local dialect and deriving most of its humor from deliberate incongruities of tone. Both liked sudden and surprise endings, though the fact that O. Henry came after Harte and before Runyon is clearly important. And, finally, both fundamentally depended on the ancient device of playing up sudden flashes of decency in people who might be considered utterly depraved—not an entirely unrealistic device, at that.[2]

As Runyon adopted some plots and stylistic devices from Bret Harte directly, he very likely was more strongly influenced by a later colleague who was also familiar with Harte's work. Alfred

Henry Lewis was a newspaperman from Kansas who wrote such Western novels as *Wolfville* (1897), *Wolfville Days* (1902), and *Wolfville Nights* (1902) before joining the *New York American*. Then Lewis adapted from the western scene to New York and published a novel about the local underworld entitled *The Apaches of New York* in 1912, just when the younger reporter was establishing himself on the same newspaper. Their styles have many similarities.

A. H. Lewis commonly used a kind of "perpetual present" tense and picturesque approach as well as favorite themes and language adapted from the works of Bret Harte. Harte's narrator interprets the characters for the readers and speaks in an elevated manner, but Lewis's and later Runyon's characters mix the slangy and ungrammatical language with some stilted and high-flown expressions. As with Mark Twain's speakers, their narrators are like the characters they describe rather than being set above them by more elevated speech patterns. Lewis combined the two styles of speaking that Harte's characters previously demonstrated. One is the Old Cattleman, a narrator who addresses the public as an insider, "speaking the Western vernacular, but with the erudite cockiness of Harte himself."[3]

Specific language uses are the most dramatic stylistic similarity between Runyon and Lewis although the latter maintains a formal, sometimes aloof descriptive pattern more like Bret Harte's when the omniscient narrator speaks instead of a minor character. For example, "That profligate, thus protected, pursued his election efforts in behalf of Mr. Updegraffe cunningly, being all unchecked."[4] A. H. Lewis's narrator appears to be involved and interested but in a minor role, more commentator than participant. He is very much a forerunner of Runyon's narrator. Whereas Runyon's language occasionally is formal or exaggerated, he less frequently has a stilted style, particularly in the later stories, and then only for occasional emphasis. Runyon contributed the simplified perspective to this literary tradition. His narrative is all in essentially the same style whether told by the primary speaker or one of the other characters.

A. Mugg, the forerunner of Runyon's Broadway narrator, like Lewis's Old Cattleman, is an insider-spectator who serves as a spokesman for the community. He aspires to cultivation and lapses into slang and errors in syntax only when he forgets himself or loses his way amid long-winded circumlocutions, "but he too acts as a kind of translator, turning the original low-life vernacular into something weirdly like refinement." Thus, the narrative style sometimes resembles Lewis's. Later Runyon's unnamed narrator has the same relationship to the Broadway world as the Old Cattleman has to Wolfville. Both are trusted insiders who know the working of their communities; but both are spectators who chiefly tell what others do. Each narrator mediates between the local community and the national audience. Additionally, both Lewis and Runyon used their underworld characters to protest against social inequity in New York City, as this example from Lewis's *The Apaches of New York* indicates.

All over New York City, in Fifth Avenue, at the Five Points, the single cry was, Get the Money! The rich were never called upon to explain their prosperity. The poor were forever being asked to give some legal reason for their poverty. Two men in a magistrate's court are fined ten dollars each. One pays, and walks free; the other doesn't, and goes to the Island. Spanish sees, and hears, and understands.

"Ah!" cries he, "that boob went to the Island not for what he did but for not having ten bones!"

And the lesson of that thunderous murmur—reaching from the Battery to Kingsbridge—Get the Money! rushes upon him; and he makes up his mind to heed it. Also, there are uncounted scores like Spanish, and other uncounted scores with better coats than his, who are hearing and seeing and reasoning the same way.[5]

Whereas Runyon adopted the present tense almost exclusively in fiction written after 1929, the origins of this style were quite varied. Entire poems and parts of short stories were written in the present tense even before he left Colorado. Though Bret Harte and A. H. Lewis may have influenced him, a more basic factor was the standard speech patterns of his uncultured associates in the schoolyard and among local families. At an early age, Runyon was sensitized to the contrast between their speech and the newspaper terminology learned at his father's knee in the local bars if not in the newsroom. On the playgrounds of Pueblo, as in the Midwest, persons with little education or culture frequently recount events of the immediate past in the present tense, such as "so I says to him when I meets him at the movies last night. . . ."

Runyon also encountered this form among hoboes, in army barracks, and amid the underworld where the language often reflected the speaker's lower-class or foreign origins. Whether out of condescension or democracy, along with the primary desire to entertain, Runyon tried to capture the bumbling and repetitive speech patterns of a less literate subculture, much as Ring Lardner satirized them as well as the dominant society. That these speech patterns had an authentic basis was verified in the Rothstein trial as well as other circumstances.

Other theories have also been offered to account for Runyon's preponderant use of the present tense. An obituary in the *Salida Daily Mail* contended that Runyon adopted the form from Joe Dinah, a steward at the Denver Press Club. Fellow newspaperman Gene Fowler gave its origins a poetic twist by suggesting that Runyon borrowed this style from Arthur Brisbane, who, in turn, acquired it from Coleridge's "Rime of the Ancient Mariner," surely a whimsical interpretation.[6]

More often, Runyon's use of the present tense has been ascribed to the writer's desire to overcome the barriers of time. Walter Winchell contended that Runyon wanted to give the reader a feeling of actually seeing the drama unfold.[7] In addition, the continued emphasis on the present and future tenses forms a protracted pun on time by diminishing its importance. Respect for the past is lessened if time has only relative value.

Runyon's style also distorts and diminishes the value of the speech patterns of the respectable middle-class society that he satirized. "The vanishing of the frontier between indicative and conditional results in a similar confusion of fact and fancy."[8] Breaking down the notion of an arbitrary and absolute reality through the use of language, the concept of time seems less consequential; and this helps reinforce Runyon's basic theme of the relativity of good and evil. In "The Old Doll's House," as was mentioned previously, the clocks are stopped at twelve o'clock for forty-five years, indicating that time may even be meaningless in some instances. A gangster uses this fact to give him an alibi for murder. Jean Wagner suggested that, in this case, the present tense also emphasizes Runyon's preoccupation with material gain, an immediate gratification.

Focusing on the present and future certainly enables the narrator and other speakers to give a piecemeal accounting of events that more or less approximates the order in which they occurred. Svend Riemer contended that Runyon's sentence structure has "a dimorphous and atomized appearance." A sense of immediate communication is derived as he strings together short sequences of nouns and verbs attached by simple addition in a flow of language characterized by "primitivism far too purposeful to be explained by the lack of mastery of the English language on the part of urban immigrant groups. . . . But the stream of words flows on, uninterrupted and with a minimum of cohesion, until it finally comes to an end by the narrator's elementary physical need of having to take a deep breath before plunging into further verbiage."[9]

Thus, Riemer concluded that Runyon's present tense and rather primitive sentence structure are a carefully wrought literary form to give this world symbolic expression, a striking adaptation of form and content that challenges the reader "when groggy from repeated shocks, to re-evaluate a pattern of life which, so far, he has taken for granted." The "primitivism" of the historical present expresses the momentary, the immediate communication, and presents a deadpan humor based on a natural fusion of form and content. Part of this stems from contrasts in Runyon's language between sophisticated and naive, over- and understatement. They shock the reader into a laugh because, finally, as Riemer saw it, Runyon's primary creativity lay in coining pert phrases and generating laughter "combined with the affectation of a complete lack of emotional concern, combined with cosmopolitan indifference that takes things for granted as they occur in the melting pot of widely heterogeneous customs, manners and mannerisms." This existential perspective corresponds with Gene Fowler's recollection of Runyon saying the present was his only reality, never the future. His literary format simply reflected Runyon's overall orientation toward life.

The first-person present tense is somewhat theatrical, but it provides continuity in a stream of experiences as well as giving a sense of immediacy and spontaneity.[10] It also summarizes—an expeditious style for the spatially limited short story. Because speech is usually in the first person, it seems like a very natural conversational form in fiction as well. Runyon's anonymous narrator maintains immediacy and keeps the action moving by integrating exposition and dialogue.

A simple viewpoint is maintained through the immediate personal continuity of the storyteller, as demonstrated in the introduction to "The Lemon Drop Kid." "I am going to take you back a matter of four or five years to an August afternoon and the race track at Saratoga. . . . On this day I am talking about, The Lemon Drop Kid is looking about for business, and not doing so good for himself at that."[11]

Sentences strung together and broken only by commas sometimes extend to the length of paragraphs and convey a sequential impression of action that reminded Jean Wagner of Walt Disney's cartoons. But the 1912 story "Nose of Nemesis" includes a chase scene that was a forerunner of "The Bloodhounds of Broadway" and also preceded Walt Disney's cartoons. Therefore, Runyon's chase scenes more likely were simply another aspect of the present-tense narrative that could be readily adapted to the motion-picture format. This example from "Little Miss Marker" demonstrates how the present and past are combined into a continual progression of time.

The Choo-Choo Boys' band in the Hot Box always play a special number for Marky in between the regular dances, and she gets plenty of applause, especially from the Broadway citizens who know her, although Henri, the manager of the Hot Box, once tells me he will just as soon Marky does not do her dancing there, because one night several of his best customers from Park Avenue, including two millionaires and two old dolls, who do not understand Marky's dancing, bust out laughing when she falls on her snoot, and Big Nig puts the slug on the guys, and is trying to put the slug on the old dolls, too, when he is finally headed off.[12]

Whatever its origins, Runyon's use of the present tense remained one of his best-known trademarks in the Broadway stories.

### Sentence Structure and Set Expressions

The local colorists added greater fidelity to the way dialect was conveyed when their tall tales were transferred to print. They recorded grammar, contractions, and homely idioms, "the authenticity of which may justify the disturbing presence of vulgarity on occasion."[13] Bret Harte focused general attention on localisms and made editors more receptive to homely, even ungenteel details of speech and manners. Similarly, Mark Twain added to the respectability of dialect by capturing the language and mores along the Mississippi. And A. H. Lewis combined local dialect with a more formal narrative style. He anticipated many of Runyon's mannerisms, ranging from certain types of understatement and euphemism to favorite adverbial constructions and catch phrases borrowed from more genteel professions. Both writers created a number of personal clichés. Lewis favored "some" and "a whole lot" while Runyon's "no little and quite some" and "more than somewhat" were trademarks.

As time went on, Runyon gradually dropped the malapropisms and misspellings as he elaborated on similes such as Lewis's "as dead as Santa Anna." Whereas A. H. Lewis tried to duplicate the sounds of speech on the printed page and contrasted this dialect with the exalted language of an omniscient narrator, Runyon substituted a collection of slang expressions that seemed like a fresh language and was easier to read. But the unified perspective and simplified language sacrificed major devices for developing distinctive individual characters. Instead, Runyon chose to emphasize the contrast between social groups.

Language is laughable because it is a human product modeled as exactly as possible on the forms of the human mind.[14] The comic absurdity engendered by the actions of characters that seem artificial, mechanical, or exaggerated can be heightened by related language. The professions become ludicrous by rigidity of language, confining the speakers to their own jargon or borrowing terms from other professions. Runyon distorts jargon like medicalese, legalese, and other borrowings from respectable professions; he also transposes them with terms from horse racing, gambling, or petty crime. Thus, men may be described as "old plugs" and women as "old haybags" while bankers may be in the "banking dodge"; and the social status of criminals may advance with their progression from petty crime to the "legitimate" business of bootlegging. By applying terminology from one profession to another, a play on words is created and amusement generated by the interaction of two independent sets of ideas. According to Henri Bergson, "A comic effect is always obtainable by transposing the natural expression of an idea into another format that recollects the old one and generates humor by a fresh setting. This humor can range from insipid buffoonery to lofty irony."[15]

By the same token, the set expressions that were so popular with Runyon's readers and so offensive to his critics have a sound basis as a comic formula. Authentic fiction strives for vivid prose pictures drawn with adjectives that add fine shades of discrimination for a more accurate portrayal. Thus, adverbs like "however" are prosaic and seldom justify the space in serious fiction.[16] Quite out of step with this trend, Runyon's highly stylized and repetitive phrases like "and all this and all that" add clutter without developing finer shades of description or meaning.

From a comic standpoint, however, the ready-made formulas and stereotyped phrases are most appropriate. Comedy thrives on repetition, and humor results from a lack of elasticity or momentum in what is said as well as done. The automation of these utterances makes the set expressions humorous. Wit is effected by combining hackneyed terms, by twisting a current idea into a paradox, or by parodying some quotation or proverb. Runyon's repetition of set expressions, slang, and the present tense creates humor in the same manner that a comedian slipping on the same banana peel more than once can be humorous to an audience that anticipates this climax. By the same token, avoiding the banana peel when the audience expects a slip can also be humorous as the unexpected varies the repetitive pattern. Bergson compares the comic repetition of words with the feeling of a repressed spring that then is released and repressed again. Word comedy is difficult to translate as humor is achieved by the structure of sentences and the choice of words as well as by lapses of attention in the language itself. Thus, a comic effect is created precisely because of the mechanical or artificial quality of Runyon's expressions.

In some cases, sentence segments are simply displaced from their usual order, such as "one little electric light burning very dim."[17] In other cases, adjectives replace adverbs or "some" is used incorrectly as an adverb: "walk past the window and look in very anxious," and "he starts to squirm around quite some."

The verbal mannerisms for which Runyon became famous generally add emphasis or replace description by generalization, such as these examples from "It Comes Up Mud": "there is no doubt that Little Alfie loves Miss Beulah Beauregard more than somewhat," "enough of her shape left to interest Mr. Paul D. Veere no little," and "he is taking her here and there, and around and about." These trademark expressions are the most distinctive feature of Runyonese along with the use of the present tense and a few common categories of terms for guns, money, and women. Like the pranks of members of the gangster subculture, they attracted readers much as viewers continue to tune in their favorite situation comedies on television because of the repetition of humor, limited character development, and small range of plots, rather than in spite of them.

### Origins of Slang

Walter Winchell understated the components of Runyonese when he contended that it was a mixture of underworld slang, Yiddish expressions, and words of his own coining. Runyon was proud of his collection of slang, which mixed terms from the underworld, including Cockney rhyming slang, with the argot of other subgroups such as hoboes, journalists, and gamblers. He also combined a few French and British words, souvenirs of trips abroad, as well as a little Yiddish from the byways of New York. Biblical terms and elegant expressions as well as some words of his own coining completed the range.

Runyon drew his slang from a variety of sources, among them the financial pages and other news, just as A. H. Lewis, a political commentator, adopted some terms from jingoistic editorials. He showed more than a superficial interest in the origins and use of language, as demonstrated in a discussion of the word "skibby" in a *New York Mirror* column of February 11, 1942.[18] And he consciously juxtaposed the terminology of different social classes, ranging from the illiterate to the highly polished. Slang contrasts with dignified language, and shoddy syntax with polished grammatical constructions that force the readers into a fresh awareness of a point of view from which they had not been accustomed to look at reality, to achieve "a vivid and realistic estimate of men and things" through his linguistic as well as social rebellion.[19]

Not concerned with the semanticists' distinction between cant, the conversational idiom of members of the specific subgroup, and jargon, their professional "shop talk," Runyon tried only to bring freshness and immediacy to his stories with terminology that was familiar to the characters he depicted. For this purpose he was willing to adopt nonce-words or "quick coinages" without concern for their legitimacy or permanence.[20] Although these terms were current at the time, some of them now seem quaintly archaic, like "hotsy totsy"; and others have become clichés, e.g., "built from the ground up."

In the 1930s critics who frowned on slang as transitory and ugly were gradually being forced to give it wider acceptance with the new emphasis on believability and authenticity in fiction, and some even contended that slang could be the "salt of the language."[21] Runyon, however, was identified as a humorist and word coiner, so he was not seriously considered an authentic adaptor of local language. Despite this, it now appears that Runyon added some appropriate slang rather the way Hemingway occasionally included a

Spanish word to indicate that the fictional conversation was ostensibly in Spanish and to give a touch of local color. Certainly, Runyon drew much of his terminology from the culture he described as he wrote about Prohibition, safecracking, racetrack touts, and others who bridged the gap between the respectable and underworld societies.

When La Rocque Du Bose analyzed 750 so-called "nonliterary words" in fifty-one of Runyon's stories, he concluded that about half came from the underworld while most of the others were colloquialisms recognizable throughout the United States in informal speech. The second-largest category, about one-sixth of the words, were general slang such as "fresh" for impudent and "pal" meaning a close friend. In addition, Du Bose concluded that a number of special slang terms were probably obtained from such fields as sports, the theater, hobo life, the carnival, and journalism. Only a few words met the classification of *Webster's New International Dictionary* as being dialect, and a few others represented the mixed speech of Americans of recent foreign extraction. Very few words were used in ways that could not be traced in special dictionaries with citations dating earlier than Runyon's period of activity.

British editors exaggerated the difference between Runyonese and standard English when they included a glossary with his works although critics still disagree on how much interpretation is needed. E. C. Bentley asserted that Runyon's vocabulary is readily intelligible, but Jean Wagner noted that a dictionary of underworld lingo is helpful to know that to "do a barber" means to talk; and that when "the old guy runs something of a sandy on Ignaz," it may be interpreted as a deception, perhaps some kind of hypnotic effect. Runyon may also complicate the interpretation by twisting the meaning of unusual terms. Jean Wagner contended that "alzo" means "the usual" or "an arrangement" instead of the original "a setup, often including bribery." In "That Ever-Loving Wife of Hymie's" the narrator concludes that ". . . 'Lasses is indeed of a nervous temperament, just as Hymie Banjo Eyes is always telling me, although up to this time I figure her nerves as the old alzo."

The original meaning is also feasible; however, as the cynical narrator assumed that 'Lasses had used her nerves as an excuse, a setup to obtain a bribe or deceive Hymie Banjo Eyes; but he changed his mind after this demonstration.

Some obscurity may have resulted because of terms that were not current outside the gangster subgroup. The underworld preserves some archaic words as well as adding new ones, and others have such limited use that they require interpretation. Although some terms are now so archaic that a glossary would be helpful, overall, rare or archaic terms are most unusual. For one thing, in most instances Runyon defined his more obscure terms in standard English, although once in awhile he would also define a slang word with another slang word, e.g., a rod, "otherwise known as a smoke-pole." Nonetheless, Murray Godwin oversimplified the issue when he said the distinguishing feature of Runyonese was that he limited himself to two tenses, the present and the future, not his use of slang. "In fact, I will go so far as to say that personally I will talk more slanguage in ten minutes as a usual thing than you will be able to find in Mr. Damon Runyon's book."[22]

In some cases, the gangster argot is mixed with that of other subgroups, more general slang, or common colloquialisms of regional or merely informal speech. Terminology is also woven in from such fields as business and finance as well as horse racing to create some farfetched metaphors and verbal parodies. While some variations on language are facetious, apparently just for the fun of it, Runyon also derived humor from euphemisms that maintain the ostensible level of refinement of the middle-class audience, an artificial social structure that his stories also satirize.

Overall, Runyon enriched the vocabulary of what Jean Wagner called "the laxity of informal conversation." To accomplish this, he generally relied on standard spellings, but he also allowed some deviation from his general framework of the present and future tenses in the personal narrative format that incorporates colorful nicknames, set expressions, colloquialisms, and occupational slang as well as the underworld argot.

## Specific Usage

Runyon occasionally won critical praise for using language that would not cause a maiden to blush. He turned this quality to advantage in euphemistic humor such as an occasional "Dee" for damn or "Aw, Filberts!" to suggest that pristine if ungrammatical language replaced more vulgar expressions. Although Runyon hinted that fiancées may not always wait to have their love consummated in marriage, sexuality is only obliquely noted—but physical attractiveness is a frequent topic. Runyon's large collection of slang was employed to describe women as well as money, guns, gambling, drinking, horses, parts of the body, and representatives of ethnic groups.

Because the basic metaphors for all levels of language depend on the five senses, many slang words refer to taste and touch, including the sense of heat and cold.[23] Food is the most popular slang image because it appeals to four of the five senses: taste, smell, sight, and touch. This image is universal among subgroups. Many standard words for food represent money in nonstandard use, e.g., dough. Others refer to people, general situations, or other matters. Food images also designate many words for drunkenness and sexual intercourse as well as parts of the body.

According to Bergson, "A comic meaning is invariably obtained when an absurd idea is fitted into a well-established phrase form."[24] Pretending to take literally an expression that was used figuratively or fixing attention on the material aspect of a metaphor makes an idea comic. Thus, comedy can be obtained from poetic metaphors such as calling waffles nonskid pancakes.[25] Runyon's female characters are often described in similar metaphors that refer to foods or flowers, c.g., cookie, waffle, tomato, strudel, or pancake. Young ones are "squab" or "fresh laid."

Much of Runyon's slang simply repeats common colloquial expressions. Thus, persons of various ethnic groups are likely to be identified by the usual range of racially derogatory terms. In some cases, Runyon simply listed these terms, a humor of disrespect ostensibly reversed. "Anyway, I have a lot of very good friends among the Italians, and I never speak of them as wops, or guineas, or dagoes, or grease balls, because I consider this most disrespectful, like calling Jewish people mockies, or Heebs, or geese." Apparently "Mustache Pete" is considered an acceptable term as the narrator uses it all the way through "Too Much Pep," and he refers to the wine as "dago red." Similarly, "Money From Home" essentially catalogues all of the usual racial slurs as a black person is variously referred to as a boogie, smudge, jig, coon, darky, smoke, dinge, and ziggaboo. Sometimes Runyon added his own variations, as when he refers to Negro children as small "stovelids."

Other terms were borrowed from ethnic groups and the Bible. As a variation on the colloquial "cops," Runyon adopted the more elegant French "gendarmes." And the Yiddish word for thief, *gonoph*, is carefully defined. Although Walter Winchell indicated that Yiddish was a major source of Runyon's slang, it more often signifies a food preference as the narrator speaks longingly of Mindy's borscht or matzo balls. Borrowings from the Bible are rare except for the humorous introduction of given names, although enemies are sometimes referred to as "Jeremiahs."

Individual terms were also borrowed randomly from numerous sources that may be obvious or obscure. Among these are "cutout" for mouth, "Irish-come-all-yeez" for songs, "ackamarakus" for false, and "stabber" for knife. From the old carnival term, cheap jewelry is described as being of "slum" poor quality. From more ancient derivations stem the words "screeve" for letter and "goril" as a gangster identified in the context of his jungle predecessor.

Other slang terms quantify with a spatial or temporal aspect, as "a chesty guy" is one who puts on airs. Similarly, Runyon described himself as "a medium boiled reporter"; and his characters extend a "medium sized" hello, perhaps a parody of Jimmy Durante's "Big Hello." As Runyon altered time by the prevailing present tense, his descriptions of age are innovative analogies. From cosmetic surgery a woman is "two face liftings old," and from horses she is "a little smooth on the tooth in the matter of age." From time she is described as "half past 38 giving her a few hours the best of it."

Much of Runyon's humor derives from individual variations of slang terms for particular things. Among those most frequently altered are names for guns. In addition to rods, betsys, and automatic roscoes, a gun might be called a pizzlo-over, old equalizer, Captain Barker, or rooty-toot-toot. In contrast, it might be daintily referred to as simply "that thing."

Runyon was similarly flexible in his handling of many terms for money within the underworld argot. Specific denominations include slugs ($1), fins or finnifs ($5), and saw bucks ($10), as well as yards ($100), half yards ($50), and Gs ($1,000). Runyon also incorporated the British shillings, pound notes, and bobs as well as such food metaphors as "potatoes," "coconuts," and "dough." Other general terms are dibs, swag, score, scratch, and ready (cash).

More poetic forms of gangster terminology were borrowed from Cockney rhyming slang. Some examples are "Simple simon on your lean and linger" (finger), "shovel and broom" (room), and "rattle and jar" (car). Runyon may also have tried his hand at improvising this form with "thirteen-and-odd," meaning the Todd Theater. He also used some pig latin, such as "umbay" for "bum" and "ellybay" for the colloquial "belly" or stomach. In Cockney rhyming argot this part of the body is the Darby Kelly.

Many terms have been confirmed as underworld terminology that seemed distinctive when Runyon used them. Thus, a "jug" is a bank, a "pete" is a safe, and a "damper" is a cash register. Sometimes the standard terms were also altered. A squealer may be referred to as a "chirper." "To put the sleeve on" meant to arrest someone while "to snatch" meant to kidnap. "Pokey" for jail more likely recalled his hobo days while "burg" for town and "drag" for street are common colloquialisms.

Among the documented underworld terms is "on the Erie," meaning to listen. Departure means "to take it on the Dan O'Leary," or in good gangster style to "duffy out of here." To leave, Runyon's characters might also "cop a sneak," "fan off," or "go on a vacation." Other possibilities are that they might "blow," "take the wind," or "take a run out powder." Runyon may have added a variation with reference to the famous track star of the 1930s when he suggested that they "take it on the Jesse Owen." He also altered "taking it on the lam" to "on the lammester" or "on the lammie." Perhaps an additional reference to farm animals was intended with this form in the Christmas story entitled "Three Wise Guys."

Like these variations, many of Runyon's pseudocoinings were really narrow distortions of terms already in existence. They were often altered by adding such suffixes as -enroo, -aroo, -ola, and -us. These endings produced expressions like "darbolas" for darbies, an old term for handcuffs; and "phonus balonus," a modification of "phony baloney," meaning false.

Instead of the colloquial "fanny" Runyon sometimes more formally referred to the buttocks as the "Francesca." More often, the level of language remains unchanged. Fighters who plan to lose fights "take a dive" or "go into the tank." They are called "watermen" or, in a more whimsical vein, "ostriches," presumably because they duck their heads and/or hide their intentions of throwing the fight.

As in his poetry, onomatopeia reproduces sounds as words. Thus, a rooty-toot-toot is a tommy gun, and "this ham hits poor old Doc Bodecker ker-bowie smack dab on the noggin." The safe crackers become weary of listening to baby John Ignatius Junior "glug-glugging" on his bottle, whereas a motor boat goes "putt-putting" through the water.

In some instances, a part is used to represent the whole. Among the synecdoches are "tongue" for lawyer and "The Beard" for Uncle Sam as a symbol of the United States. Similarly, the Bible is called "the Gideon" in acknowledgment of the publisher who distributes this book to hotel rooms.

Simply varying common terms also invokes humor, as with "nod guy" (yes man), "in the sachel" (bag), or "pair of tops" (loaded dice). In some cases, both the verb and its object are colloquial, e.g., "start up heat" (pressure), "chill a beef" (settle an argument), "chew the fat" (talk), "cop a sneak" (leave without being noticed), or "play the duck for him" (avoid him).

Perhaps Runyon came close to actual word coining with adjectives turned into nouns. He referred to a woman as a "gorgeous" or a "beautiful," but he most likely adopted this terminology from society pages of the newspapers where it was common. Society columnist Cholly Knickerbocker wrote about "the fashionables," and a story is headlined "Elegantes to Attend Revue to Aid Charity."[26] According to Ed Weiner, Runyon did coin the term "Komoppo," which he defined as a lady who flaunts her wealth. He derived "Chinee" for complimentary tickets because, like Chinese money, they have holes punched in them.[27] Runyon gave these explanations to censors, who then let the words remain in the movie version of "Butch Minds the Baby."[28] Nor have the backgrounds been traced for "blouwzola" or "old Chromo," presumably terms Runyon also invented.

If the meaning is not clear from the context, confusion may arise because some of Runyon's terms mean more than one thing. In many cases one meaning has more finality than the other. A "marker" may be either an IOU or a tombstone. To "give someone the chill" may mean either to slight or to kill him. And "to knock off" may mean to kill or to eat. To "guzzle" also has an extreme disparity of meanings, either to kill or to kiss. A "belt" may be a pleasure or a blow, but seldom an item of apparel. A "kick" may be a thrill or a pocket while a "taw" is a new beginning or a supply of money, often representing the same thing. While "do-re-mi" may simply extend the term "dough" as a food analogy for money, its musical origins also are appropriate to describe a fighter who does "the old do-re-mi," or in other words dances instead of fights.

Combining disparate terms gives a fresher insight because they are not usually together. Runyon's language is more vivid because of such expressions as "a two handed spender," "a sure footed doctor," and "drinking single handed." Other terms now seem simply shopworn, such as "to put the Indian sign on Brooklyn," to indicate being sure of beating that baseball team, and "to put water on Aikin's wheel," meaning to play into his hand.

Images that include a verb are often more vivid. A slow fighter "never had much foot," and an unreceptive woman "plays the ice for a man." A waitress "deals them off her arm," and we have all been "troubled with the shorts as regards dough." To be friendly is to "play the warm for someone," and "to put in with" is to agree or go along with another person. A character traveling fast may be "busting along" (speeding) in a "short" (taxi). To understand is to be "jerry to" something, and to reminisce is to "cut up old touches." Similarly, one who puts on airs may "chuck quite a swell," "play plenty of swell for him," or be a "chesty" guy.

Some of Runyon's comparisons are modifications of trite expressions, e.g., "his face was as white as a fresh collar," and a cat was "as black as a yard up a chimney." Others fall into the category of clichés, as when the "hot horse turns out to be as cold as a landlord's heart," and "she has an ice cream cone for a heart." Others exaggerate in the manner of the western tall tale. For instance, "the horse has enough lather to shave the House of David." Some images or their derivations are more oblique, such as "Katie-bar-the-door" to indicate the end of a story. It is difficult to assess Baseball Hattie's mood when she is "as happy as nine dollars worth of lettuce"; presumably in the Depression this was an indication of quantity rather than cost.

In some cases the metaphors are more complex. Runyon's tough guys are "lumbered and sent to college," probably a reflection of their hardness or strength, like trees, and the advanced criminal education they receive in prison. To be tattooed or crocheted with a gun is a readily apparent image. But Runyon also drew a more extended picture, as when Haystack Duggeler "takes a paralyzed oath" that he will reform. Jean Wagner contended that this metaphor means to swear on a Bible with an arm so straight as to signify paralysis, an appropriate description of what is needed for Haystack to have credibility in light of his extensive reputation for larceny. Runyon also applied the original meaning of "parasol" as a shadow to signify the ghost or imitation of a prize fighter. The term also relates to an umbrella as a fighter who quickly folds up.

Metaphors are also combined with puns, so that a bad play, a smeller, is called "dramatic halitosis." And Runyon punned on "hot" regarding a criminal wanted by the law. Big Jule has such a long criminal record that Runyon called him "the hottest guy in the world" and "practically on fire." The narrator wishes to avoid Jule because "I do not care to have hot guys around me, or even guys who are only just a little bit warm."

The comic effect is also varied by transposing the extreme ends of language, solemn and familiar. Mixing elevated and substandard language generates humor by contrast. For instance, elevated language is appropriate but excessively formal for Mr. Phillip Randolph, a Harvard man who says that "there is the chap who rebuffs me so churlishly on the train when I offer him our colors." This stilted style stands out as an even more humorous incongruity compared with the language of lower-class characters.

Some of Runyon's incorrect usage appears to be added facetiously to achieve another dimension of somewhat colloquial linguistic humor. Among these expressions are double plurals, e.g., "bootses" and "pantses"; and double past participles, e.g., "drunked up," "pleasured up," or "sored up." Wagner suggested that some expressions are reminiscent of western dialect, e.g., "plumb wore out" and the use of "where" and "what" for "that": "There is no doubt but what Grafton will be placed under observation long ago." The use of "dast" may also be in this category, or it may be an attempt at contrast by a slightly elevated tone.

Upon careful analysis, then, the wording of Runyonese involves a collection of slang and colloquial terms mixed with standard English in a range from familiar to lofty. The prevailing feature is the ongoing narrative that mixes direct and reported speech with immediacy and continuity primarily because the speaker favors the present and future tenses. This forces the reader into a greater awareness of language and a more intense involvement with the stories.

## Chapter Nine

# Damon Runyon in Retrospect

### Slanguage: Evaluation

Even before the end of his lifetime, critics complained that Run-yonese was dated and repetitive. The most striking aspect of Damon Runyon's short stories, however, now, as when they were first pub-lished, is his distinctive "slanguage." During the first part of the 1930s, as collected editions of his short stories were published, the reviewers tended to accept the proclamations of linguistic authen-ticity by Heywood Broun and Walter Winchell in the introductions to *Guys and Dolls* and *Blue Plate Special*.

Winchell insisted that Runyon himself talked like his characters, and Gene Fowler substantiated this to some extent, but others dis-agreed. Howard Lindsay and Leonard Lyons said no one on Broad-way talked like the small-time hoods in these stories. Runyon felt compelled to defend himself in 1933 when W. J. Funk included him among "the ten most fecund makers of the American slang then current." Runyon protested that he did not invent but only reported the language of his characters.[1] Despite his objections, Runyon re-mained on the list of word coiners in H. L. Mencken's *The Amer-ican Language* although the 1948 edition noted that Runyon had rejected this identification. This kettle came to full boil in England in 1937 when the *London Evening Standard* began publishing one of Runyon's short stories each day. The series began with praise of the stories on the front page, printed glowing biographical sketches of Runyon, and proudly published the fiction with gangster woodcuts on the center double spread.

The stories were so popular that the author became an immediate celebrity in Great Britain: His characters' language was so widely imitated that some critics voiced fears that Runyon had jeopardized the King's English. Since he had borrowed some expressions from British slang, this turnabout seems appropriate. Lord Beaverbrook, however, soon became aware that he had purchased a donnybrook along with the newspaper rights to *More Than Somewhat*, the British edition of *The Best of Runyon*. The British were not so much concerned about whether or not Americans actually spoke like Runyon's characters as that the newspaper should uphold the forms of language in standard dictionaries against invaders like Runyon who took such liberties with the King's English.

When H. K. Hales wrote in a letter to the editor that it was "indecent" to call a lady a "moll" and a gentleman a "guy," he also contended that the great British dailies should uphold the tradition of good English. This brought a deluge of letters on both sides of the controversy and Runyon's greatest praise. G. D. R. Planton went so far as to say: "Seriously, though in a minor sphere, Runyon is comparable to Shakespeare and Milton as an improvisator of language. Runyon should be rated a genius for breaking so much new ground."[2]

When *Furthermore* was published in England, the *London Times* critic reassured readers that "runyonese" was not likely to undermine the English language. Despite all of the "runyon-carriers" in the United States, there had been no great epidemic of "runyonese." In fact, he contended that Runyon was not likely to have any more influence than the literary style of Anita Loos's *Gentlemen Prefer Blondes*. While Runyon's historic present tense may represent the speech of citizens of foreign origin in some of the poorer sections of New York, this reviewer indicated that Runyon primarily invented an argot suited to the fantastic people and events that he depicted.[3] A year later, a review of *Take It Easy* suggested that the extraordinary and somewhat exaggerated enthusiasm accorded the earlier volumes, *More Than Somewhat* and *Further-*

*more*, was in the nature of a seven days' wonder and had subsided. The critic said Runyonese no longer influenced dealings on the Stock Exchange, "which may lead to a weakening in the market for Mr. Runyon's new stories."

Not surprisingly, in the furor Runyon's stories touched off in Great Britain, some of the letters to the editor also imitated Runyonese. In 1937, J.F.L. of St. Helens, Lancashire, pointed out to the editor of the *Spectator* that critics gave E. C. Bentley's edition of *The Best of Runyon* belated recognition because some individual stories and a collected edition had been published in England as early as 1932. J.F.L. noted that one reviewer finally recognized Runyon's talent and compared him with Homer. "Now when Mr. Bentley's book comes off it seems that several of the scribes become more excited than somewhat about Mr. Runyon, whom some of them compare with a guy by the name of Homer, and although up to this time I have as close an acquaintance with Homer as I have with an Eskimo's sun-bonnet, which is no acquaintance whatever, I get to figuring that he must certainly be a prominent scribbler if he is discussed with Mr. Runyon, and so I mention the matter to a literary friend of mine." J.F.L. concluded that Homer "cannot be so dumb, at that," and indicated his pleasure that Runyon was finally recognized, although he heard "that Mr. Runyon's true reward is such as will make the seventh heaven look like a postman's share of a consolation prize."[4]

E. C. Bentley also responded in Runyonese, but only to acknowledge prudently that "a guy named Jarrold" had indeed published some of Runyon's stories in England in 1932. He speculated that the time had not been right for them to receive critical recognition then. "But I do not mention these facts in my introduction to *More Than Somewhat* because I figure it is a tough break for the Jarrold guy when he published this book, and the newspapers and the public do not give it much of a tumble; and I do not see where it is any of my put-in to go raking up unhappy memories."[5]

Although their enthusiasm was waning by 1940, in a column that paid tribute to Runyon as he celebrated his fortieth year as a newspaperman, *Time Magazine* noted that Runyon's prose still had a peculiar fascination for Britons. "Five volumes of Runyon short stories have been gobbled up in Britain, South Africa, Australia, New Zealand. London's cockneys and duchesses glibly repeat Runyon's Broadwayese, talking tough, from the corners of their mouths." But the constant repetition of the same format wore down the reviewers more than any concern over authenticity. In 1944 Phillip Van Doren concluded that reading Runyon's unvarying style "is to hear echoes of the recent past." Van Doren, however, went on to find fault with the work of James T. Farrell and to conclude that the American short story overall was in a rut.[6]

When Clark Kinnaird published *Runyon First and Last* in 1949, he expressed the major fear that Runyonese would date the Broadway stories so that their "satanic" humor might become obscure. And in reviewing this book, John Lardner concluded that Runyon was a successful commercial alloy, an author who refused to repeat the language of Broadway to which his ear was carefully tuned.

Runyon's linguistic veracity was given more credibility in the early 1950s when Spiller and his associates described *Guys and Dolls* as "the first of several volumes which told in illiterate, imaginative slang about the adventures of gamblers and other sporting characters of the big city." Runyon's more genial tone was unfavorably contrasted, however, with Ring Lardner's "savage mimicry and slang."

After that, semanticists like David W. Maurer, La Rocque Du Bose, and Jean Wagner somewhat restored Runyon's reputation as an adapter of language who coined very few words, although "a host of his tropes might be considered quasi-coinings of various degrees." The charge that Runyon wrote "illiterate slang" was refuted with Wagner's argument that if there is no literate slang, there can be no such thing as illiterate slang. Instead the semanticists concluded that Runyon's colorful language was primarily adapted from several subgroups, particularly the argot of the criminal, but with some individual modifications. Authenticating the origins of Runyon's language and use of the present tense only accounted for one dimension of his style. The distinctly Runyonese modifications of language, plot, and character were still the basis of his popularity.

### The Short-Story Format

During the twenty years when Damon Runyon was perfecting his complex and colorful writing techniques, the masters of the short story were altering the accepted format in a somewhat different direction. In the 1920s both Sherwood Anderson and Ernest Hemingway hit their stride in writing spare, taut fiction while Runyon achieved fame as a newspaper reporter; but he was still collecting rejection slips from magazines for his short-story efforts.

Mark Twain and Bret Harte had prepared the way for a closer representation of the spoken language in fiction. Then Anderson and Hemingway further developed the stream of experience style. They let description and conversation flow naturally without interference by formal punctuation, whether in indirect discourse or direct dialogue.[7] After World War I American writers used the local vernacular as their literary language, trying to keep it as close to life and the senses as possible to recreate experience, sensation, and the apprehension of reality.[8]

The goal toward which fiction writers strove was to maintain the illusion of life's progression. Good stories were expected to maintain an intensity of emotion and singleness of impact that would increase with the continuously specific dramatic action in the immediate sequence. For this purpose, the author acquaints the reader only with the details that have unique application to the particular person, place, and time. Thus, a good short-story plot reduces the complex multiplicity of experience into a clear, logical pattern. To accomplish this, the central focus can revolve around the action or the character. Either may give vitality to the other.

Despite the emphasis on plain prose that made Hemingway more popular than Faulkner and confined Runyon to a critical Siberia, the so-called revolt from the village depicted in American literature between world wars retained much of the small-town language and local color. Thus, the most simple style was not always the most authentic, the basic requirement of American fiction. Narrative prose had to have a range of levels from the vulgar to the elegant, and vagueness could sometimes make a story more believable and interesting. As the best stories grow out of real or possible life experience, the best language is controlled by plot and point of view with varying styles among characters who show their individuality by speaking differently. In addition, the best narrative prose has a spontaneous, headlong quality that seems natural rather than planned. Thus, the predominant qualities of modern American prose have been described as movement, speed, and sensation.

But the key remains authenticity as critics contend that writing is a form of self-realization, "a mania for mimesis." Although the good writer unites event, language, content, and form, cumbersome and even downright awkward writing styles have also been tolerated in the name of authenticity. For instance, Sinclair Lewis and Sherwood Anderson piled on details of external reality in portrayals of small-town life, while Theodore Dreiser and Richard Wright incorporated whole newspaper columns practically verbatim. The painful struggle for self-identity in the black subculture inhibited Richard Wright's protagonists while the boredom and trivia of small-town life and lower-class values gave the novels by Sinclair Lewis and Theodore Dreiser a ring of authenticity.

In some ways, however, the desire for simplicity came into conflict with the struggle for authenticity. As Leon Surmelian noted, "in fiction there is room for all kinds of style, the simple and ornate, the natural and artificial, the direct and the oblique, the metaphoric and cinematic." Perhaps their veracity was reinforced as fictional depictions of pettiness and greed engendered hostility among the residents of places like Anderson's Clyde, Ohio; Dreiser's Terre Haute, Indiana; Lewis's Sauk Centre, Minnesota; and even Wright's Natchez, Mississippi, to some extent. In contrast, Damon Runyon's humor entertained his readers, made him popular with the home folks, and generally kept him one step away from the battles over fictional authenticity.

Other writers were able to compromise the quest for fictional authenticity in various ways. For one thing, American readers are accustomed to accept exaggerated styles such as the headlines of newspapers and the tall tales by Mark Twain and other burlesque humorists. Extravagant and dramatic language is tolerated better than abstractions. Works like Stephen Crane's "The Open Boat" are favored for the concrete detail that gives them a physical, sensuous impact. "Good narrative prose abounds in concrete nouns, active verbs, qualifying adjectives (in moderation), and the first person pronoun I."[9] But critics were unable to accept Runyon's satirical humor as part of this tradition anymore than they could relate his repetitive style to the serious art contributed by Anderson and Hemingway.

In some respects, however, Runyon does demonstrate techniques that relate to Anderson's and Hemingway's. They extended their literary raw material to characters and subjects previously regarded as subliterary and inappropriate. Both broke through the stereotypes to create their own distinctive topics and styles. In the same way Runyon carried this further by presenting the underdog's perspective through the racetrack and gangster subcultures. Nonetheless, the underlying issue regarding Runyon's short fiction is whether or not he presented authentic characters, situations, and language.

H. E. Bates noted that the highly individualistic styles of writers like Anderson and Hemingway led to the danger of unconscious parody of themselves.[10] As time went on, Hemingway's style became more traditional in recognition of this problem; but Runyon continued to write in the same format. Thus, his stories more and more seemed like parodies of themselves. "Romance in the Roaring Forties" presented a setting, formula, cast of characters, and style that Runyon modified only slightly over the next decade and a half.

Despite their lower standing now, when the collected editions of Runyon's short stories and columns were published, they were widely, seriously, and often favorably reviewed along with the works of authors like Thomas Wolfe and James T. Farrell. Each new edition of stories brought Runyon laurels as one of America's most popular writers. At the same time they reinforced the critics' contention that he was too repetitive. In 1938 the *London Times* critic saw little variety in Runyon's plots and characters; "and his verbal fantasies, however surprising and peculiar, vary little from one story to the next." Lisle Bell was an exception when he categorized *Take It Easy* as a sparkling assortment of plots and contended that Runyon's characters were taken from an undiminished reservoir. "The haunts are familiar—Saratoga, Miami, Broadway, Brooklyn—but the facts (roughly speaking) are as fresh as this morning's eggs." In 1939 Runyon's first three books, *Guys and Dolls*, *Blue Plate Special*, and *Money From Home*, were reissued as *The Damon Runyon Omnibus*. This evoked another round of the criticisms of the original volumes: that the plots pivot on sentiment, coincidence, or both, and that they include some "venerable platitudes."[11]

Reviewers frequently compared Runyon's stories with fairy tales. Murray Godwin said the Cinderella quality appealed to people's yearning for romance. Runyon reinforced this superficial image by agreeing that he wrote variations on the tales of Cinderella and Snow White.[12] While probably said tongue-in-cheek, this remark was widely repeated and encouraged critics to treat him strictly as a humorist and disregard the social criticism. The *London Times* reviewer contended that Runyon's characters are sufficiently far removed from any reality known to an English reader to belong to fairyland.[13]

American reviewers expressed the same opinion when *Runyon First and Last* was published in 1949. Meyer Berger contended that "the characters say and do things that no Broadway lug ever dreamed of doing or saying, but you can love them or hate them as you hated the characters in Hans Christian Andersen."[14] John Lardner also concluded that Runyon's stories were Cinderella dreams written by a practicing cynic with an obvious grasp of the betting odds against Cinderella, "a man who produced romance at so many coconuts a word."[15] Lardner concluded that Runyon's stories took on a queer, mixed flavor because he finally joined his scores of imitators and imitated himself in the last Broadway stories, repeating and exploiting the synthesis he had created.

Indeed, some parallels with fairy tales can be drawn. They also deal with love and violence and frequently have rather simple story lines and an absence of psychological depth. In addition, as most of the critical attention was focused on the underworld society in itself rather than in comparison with the dominant society, J. C. Furnas noted that "almost invariably the fundamental principle is the reasonably well-worn device of making a hard-boiled enemy of society behave like St. Francis of Assisi, demonstrating for all and sundry that the softest hearts beat beneath the latest fashions in bullet-proof vests."[16] Not everyone agreed. Given the attraction of the underworld, however, quite likely the violence was more acceptable if placed in the context of fairy tales rather than reality.

Even Clark Kinnaird repeated Furnas's comment in the Foreword to *Runyon First and Last*, seeming to need some justification for the hoodlums' behavior even though he also quotes Runyon's cynical remark that "there are only three men in the night life of Broadway whose word is worth a nickel." Kinnaird contended that Runyon's favorite characters were the Turps and My Old Man, especially the former, whom he delineates as "basic Americans with all the homely and broad virtues." With this bow to traditions of literary acceptability, Kinnaird seemed to have a rationale for enjoying the Broadway stories. "Understanding this, we may enjoy the gargantuan humor of the *comédie humaine* he lays in Broadway, without any afterfeelings of shame for having laughed at the crimes, violence, dissipation and predatory worthlessness of most of his Broadway people. We may begin to appreciate the quality of his craftsmanship."

Critics seemed to need to separate the violence from reality in order to enjoy the humor. They then charged Runyon with a false depiction of the world despite some realistic aspects. John Lardner contended that Runyon traveled a street approximately parallel with reality but three or four blocks removed.[17] For Fletcher Pratt, however, the success of Runyon's stories depended on their fidelity to the subject. He could not account for it by anything in the catalogue of qualities such as plots that depend on sentiment, coincidence, or the Broadway background and dialect. Instead, one factor, according to Pratt, may be the way Runyon reproduced the rhythms of speech and life in a special world.

There is, in fact, an underlying fidelity to the subject in his work; a fidelity missing from the ordinary cheap magazine stories with which his seem to belong. This becomes clear from an examination not of the central themes of the stories in this collection, but of the details that surround them. . . . Gangster and cop may save each other's lives in a moment of emotional reflex, but in the next moment each is thinking how he can best cash in on the other's gratitude. Evil is quite apt to prosper like the green bay tree—or rather there is no such thing as evil, there is only life, in a bewildering maze of manifestations without any absolute standards.[18]

Not long after Runyon's death, Svend Riemer picked up the cry that Runyon was an objective journalist who did not moralize at all. "He accepts the assignment and gives an adequate account of the individuals who strive to find meaning amid the complex and isolating forces of modern urban life." Riemer took seriously Runyon's contention that he confined himself to variations on the theme of Cinderella but contended that he managed to inject a basis for realism by the fact that the glorified sentiment of the melodrama "is bearable only because it is diluted by tough and hard humor." In effect, Riemer contended that Runyon's characters are authentic within a modern world that is absurd or artificial.

The indifference of the cosmopolitan atmosphere, "a highly artificial and inhuman environment," contrasts with the continuous reassertion of human nature, the sentimental yearnings of the characters. This reassertion, Riemer says, is the eternal theme of the Runyon short story. Thus, Runyon is portrayed as a spokesman for urban life, a kind of modern regionalism that may reflect the growing popularity of a range of literature that "explores the environmental background of this continent as a stage setting for urbanism" in which Runyon crystallizes attitudes associated with "human helplessness in a complex and artificial environment—made by man and yet not mastered—if urbanism suggests the paradox of solitude in milling crowds and that of sentimental yearning in a highly rationalized machine culture . . . then Damon Runyon has laid his finger on a central theme of our present civilization."[19] This sophisticated analysis gave Runyon credit for more depth and social purpose than the humorist likely intended.

## Literary and Social Status

After his death in 1946, Runyon continued to be highly respected among his fellow sports reporters. In 1950 Jack MacDonald contended that he would still be most likely to be named the century's best sports writer even against such noteworthy and, in some cases, still living competitors as Grantland Rice, Bill McGeehan, Westbrook Pegler, and old friend turned antagonist, Paul Gallico.[20] That same year a hit musical comedy, *Guys and Dolls*, returned the spirit of Runyon to Broadway. It was based on three of Runyon's short stories: "The Idyll of Miss Sarah Brown," "Blood Pressure," and "Pick the Winner." Since then, summer-stock audiences have continued to delight in such characters as Sky Masterson and Nathan Detroit, who runs the longest continuous floating crap game in New York City. After a movie adaptation starring Marlon Brando as Sky Masterson, this resurgence of interest resulted in new editions of many of Runyon's works in the United States and Great Britain as well as a television series based on his short stories. Most of these new editions were published before 1960. Eventually they totalled twenty-two American, thirteen British, and at least nine foreign-language publications in Dutch, French, Indonesian, and Italian.[21]

Despite this immense popularity, critical analyses of short-story writing techniques only briefly mentioned Runyon in the 1940s and 1950s, more often to acknowledge his popularity than to analyze his style. Thus, aside from a very few articles tracing influences on Runyon's fiction, it was left to linguists like David W. Maurer, La Rocque Du Bose, and finally Jean Wagner to assess Runyon's language, style, and authenticity more comprehensively. *Runyonese: The Mind and Craft of Damon Runyon* by French critic Jean Wagner is the only book-length evaluation of his work as part of the serious craft of writing fiction.

Runyon's fame as a newspaper reporter has, overall, evoked more reminscences and critical evaluations. The first two biographies, Ed Weiner's *The Damon Runyon Story* (1948) and Damon Runyon, Jr.'s, *Father's Footsteps* (1954), subjectively chronicled the author's life. It was left to Edwin P. Hoyt, however, to write a more objective and comprehensive biography. His *A Gentleman of Broadway* (1964) destroyed many of the myths but left intact Runyon's reputation as a newspaper reporter and humorist.

The books by Edwin P. Hoyt and Jean Wagner are the only extended, serious attempts to assess Runyon's writing style and subject matter, their origins, or his literary influence. Hoyt surveyed major libraries in the United States in the early 1960s and determined that Runyon was still popular among general readers. Although five collections of his short fiction were listed in the *Wilson Fiction Catalogue* of 1960, Hoyt noted that only a handful of college and university professors discussed his stories in their classes. Instead, "the name of Damon Runyon seemed to arouse some academicians to fury." Among them was an English teacher at a midwestern university who called Runyon a bad writer and termed Runyonese "an artsy craftsy hoax on language."[22] Hoyt observed that most of Runyon's critics judged him despite very limited familiarity with his works. Many acknowledged not even knowing about the existence of Runyon's three volumes of verse or the early short stories published in *Runyon First and Last*.

Jean Wagner theorized that Runyon's fiction had not been accepted as an authentic representation of society because most critics misread his intent. They missed the social satire by perceiving him only as a comedian because of attention focused on the gangster subculture and his lightness of tone. This suggested that he was "fit only to entertain." Wagner also contended that detective stories were accepted as reality, so the critics were reluctant to acknowledge Runyon's well-documented social record of the underworld. In contrast, Runyon saw the detective story as an effort by respectable people to reinforce the classifications of individuals into the good and bad categories that he was attempting to break down.

While many of the academicians' objections to Runyon are on solid ground in terms of the contemporary literary standard for short fiction, he has a more valid claim to recognition as a humorist and social satirist to be compared with James Thurber or Ring Lardner. The fact that Runyon did not write any serious fiction or lecture on his techniques of formulating humor probably limited his claim to serious critical evaluation along with the fact that he published in newspapers and popular magazines instead of in the *New Yorker*.

Although serious critics perceive Runyon's style as being "as dead as a doornail, maybe deader," as with some other Americans who generated interest abroad as well, the enthusiasm for Runyon's prose continued longer in other countries, notably Great Britain. Anthony Burgess acknowledged Runyon's short story "A Piece of Pie" as the inspiration for the eating contest in *Tremor of Intent* and, more importantly, that Runyon's language motivated him to create his own version of Lancashire "rocker" slang for *A Clockwork Orange*.[23] Moreover, the early 1970s brought *Guys and Dolls* back to Broadway with an all-black cast. This was followed by another movie version of "Little Miss Marker," and by Tom Clark's *The World of Damon Runyon*, which recalls something of his life and times.

From an historical perspective, Runyon's later short stories also warrant attention as a minor but socially significant chronicle of the language and mores of the gangland subculture in itself. His background, personal friendships, and professional associations as a sports and crime reporter qualified the newsman to be a spokesman for this subculture. While newspapers familiarized their readers with front-page accounts of gangster activities, Runyon fictionalized the personal foibles of these fringe members of society. His short stories placed them in a context that could be interpreted and accepted by the general public. This was noted in 1942 when Kunitz and Haycraft called him "the prose laureate of the semi-literate American." While emphasizing his role as a newspaper reporter, they contended that readers were captivated by "his humor, his realistic view of human nature and his inexhaustible spirit. His style is frequently journalistic, and if he attains no other immortality, his books will someday be an invaluable source for the study of current American speech."[24]

Runyon translated underworld language and attitudes into somewhat believable as well as humorous conflicts between social and antisocial forces. The initial readers may have missed the satire on the larger society as they read Runyon's stories to escape the realities of the Great Depression and World War II. They gloried in the language, contrived plots, colorful characters, and happy endings undercut by cynicism as well as the fantasies of beating the law, finding true love, or simply putting one over on the other guy. This represented a small triumph for the underdog or at least a manifestation of the sense of isolation felt by those in the mainstream as well as outside it. The Broadway stories convey an additional level of social insight by satirizing common values within the larger society and by juxtaposing it against one subculture. Thus, Runyon can be recognized appropriately as a minor but legitimate social critic and humorist. His claim to fame rests primarily on his creation of a distinctive style of writing, vocabulary, and cast of colorful characters that comment on the prevalent society in an entertaining manner.

While Runyon's popularity initially rested on his contemporary way of entertaining his readers, he also continued an older literary tradition. The gangster as an American folk hero enhances and extends the mystique of the Western cowboy and gunslinger. They were being romanticized as folk heroes in Colorado before Runyon applied this Western literary tradition to the subculture of New York gangland society. The American cities bore some resemblance to the lawless frontier during Prohibition when bootleggers were accepted as colorful characters by a society in rebellion against its own laws. The fact that nostalgia and other sentiments are undercut by a strong current of cynicism gives some aspects of Runyon's stories a quite contemporary flavor, however.

Runyon's early satires on the romance and local color of the pioneers and Indians of the West were appropriate forerunners of what now are reminiscences of the good old days of Prohibition. Runyon noted that the gangsters themselves were reminiscing by 1934.[25] Movie depictions like Edward G. Robinson's famous portrayal of a gangster in the movie *Little Caesar* were followed by television programs like "The Untouchables," narrated by Runyon's old friend Walter Winchell. They demonstrate the beachhead that westerner Runyon established on the sidewalks of New York. He romanticized and satirized the sports, racing, and underworld crowds as part of the American heritage along with the pioneering spirit that drew his forebears from the East to Manhattan, Kansas. Runyon simply reversed Horace Greeley's famous adage: "Go West Young Man, Go West," when the tides of opportunity turned the other way. His gangster society, like the earlier Western traditions, has now become the subject for nostalgia buffs.

Runyon described basic aspects of human nature and interactions, somewhat in the manner of Norman Rockwell. Both of them were able to depict slightly romanticized, humorous versions of the local Everyman. Runyon could generate more interest in the neighbors' domestic squabbles than some accounts of winning sports competitions or waging wars described by others less endowed with the power of the pen. The continued popularity of the musical *Guys and Dolls* also suggests the ongoing appeal of Runyon's portraits of small-time hoods and racetrack hangers-on, the fringe element of society. These outsiders continue to interest middle-class audiences, part of the larger society that Runyon also satirized with his gangster microcosm.

# Notes and References

## Chapter One

1. Edwin P. Hoyt, *A Gentleman of Broadway* (Boston, 1964), p. 28.
2. Anon., "Runyon, Damon," *Current Biography*, 1942, n.v., p. 724.
3. William Hebert, "For Damon, October 4, 1884–December 10, 1946," n.d., Damon Runyon Memorial Fund for Cancer Research, Inc., p. 4.
4. Walter Winchell, untitled tribute to Damon Runyon, n.p., n.d., Damon Runyon Memorial Fund for Cancer Research, Inc.
5. Walter Blair, *Native American Humor* (San Francisco: Chandler Publishing Co., 1969), p. 148.

## Chapter Two

1. Blair, p. 18.
2. Svend Riemer, "Damon Runyon—Philosopher of City Life," *Social Forces*, 25 (May 1947): 402.
3. Ernest Hemingway, *Green Hills of Africa* (New York: Charles Scribner's Sons, 1953), p. 22.
4. Samuel Langhorne Clemens, *Adventures of Huckleberry Finn: An Annotated Text, Backgrounds and Sources, Essays in Criticism* (New York: W. W. Norton and Co., 1962), p. 83.
5. Damon Runyon, "The Informal Execution of Soupbone Pew," in *Runyon First and Last*, ed. Clark Kinnaird (Philadelphia, 1949), p. 115.
6. Damon Runyon, "My Father," in *Runyon First and Last*, p. 135.

## Chapter Three

1. Jean Wagner, *Runyonese: The Mind and Craft of Damon Runyon* (Paris, 1965), p. 45.

2. Hoyt, p. 190.

3. Damon Runyon, "On Good Turns," in *My Old Man* (New York, 1939), p. 42.

4. Damon Runyon, "Dr. Davenport," in *In Our Town* (New York, 1946), p. 75.

5. John Nichol, *American Literature, an Historical Sketch* (Edinburgh: Adam and Charles Black, 1885), p. 426.

6. Anon., "The Essence of Runyon," *Newsweek*, May 20, 1946, p. 71.

7. Damon Runyon, "Hank Smith," in *In Our Town*, p. 120.

8. Damon Runyon, "Says Damon Runyon: Masterson—A Real Man," *New York American*, October 26, 1921, p. 9.

9. Damon Runyon, "Lou Louder," in *More Guys and Dolls* (New York, 1951), p. 53.

10. Ibid., p. 56.

11. Wagner, p. 143.

12. Kenneth Payson Kempton, *The Short Story* (Cambridge, Mass.: Harvard University Press, 1967), pp. 110–12.

13. Damon Runyon, "The Wisdom of Not Being Wise," in *Short Takes: Readers' Choice of the Best Columns of America's Favorite Newspaperman* (New York, 1946), p. 9.

*Chapter Four*

1. Damon Runyon, "Damon Runyon Reports the Ruth Snyder–Judd Gray 'Dumbell Murder' Case," in *A Treasury of Great Reporting: "Literature Under Pressure" from the Sixteenth Century to Our Time*, ed. Lewis L. Snyder and Richard B. Morris (New York: Simon and Schuster, 1962), p. 439.

2. Hoyt, p. 167.

3. Dan Parker, "Damon Runyon Dies: Top Hearst Writer," *Editor and Publisher* 79 (December 14, 1946): 83.

4. Snyder and Morris, p. xxix.

5. Damon Runyon, "Wind Storm," in *Short Takes*, p. 12.

6. Murray Schumach, "Mr. Runyon's Blue Plate Specials," *New York Times*, June 2, 1946, p. 27.

7. Anon., "The Essence of Runyon," *Newsweek*, May 20, 1946, p. 71.

8. Anon., "Runyon with the Half-Boob Air," *Time,* June 24, 1946, p. 70.

9. Damon Runyon, "Magnificent Mammon," in *Short Takes,* p. 56.

10. Hoyt, p. 18.

11. Damon Runyon, "The Eternal Blonde," in *Trials and Other Tribulations* (Philadelphia, 1947), p. 163.

12. Ibid., p. 175.

13. Anon., "Runyon: Sports Writer Chafes in His Former Chief's Mantle," *News-Week,* January 16, 1937, p. 35.

14. Damon Runyon, *The Turps,* "Publisher's Note" (London, 1951), p. 6.

15. Anon., "American Lives," *London Times Literary Supplement,* December 2, 1939, p. 702.

16. Damon Runyon, "Nothing Happens in Brooklyn," in *More Guys and Dolls,* p. 242.

17. Damon Runyon, "The Hottest Guy in the World," in *The Damon Runyon Omnibus* (Garden City, N.Y., 1944), p. 130.

18. Damon Runyon, "A Call on the President," in *More Guys and Dolls,* p. 246.

*Chapter Five*

1. Damon Runyon, *Poems for Men,* ed. Clark Kinnaird (Garden City, N.Y., 1951), p. xi.

2. Leo Kennedy, "Poems for Men," *Chicago Sun,* December 15, 1947, p. 33.

3. Damon Runyon, "The Song of the Strike Breakers," in *The Tents of Trouble* (New York, 1911), p. 25.

4. Damon Runyon "John Barleycorn, John Barleycorn!" in *Poems for Men,* p. 30.

5. William Flint Thrall and Addison Hibbard, *A Handbook to Literature,* revised and enlarged by C. Hugh Holman (New York: Odyssey Press, 1960), p. 42.

6. Damon Runyon, "Officer and Gentleman," in *Rhymes of the Firing Line* (New York, 1912), p. 46.

7. Damon Runyon, "Christmus at Jakey's Place," *Denver Times Friday Magazine,* December 23, 1904, p. 4.

8. Damon Runyon, "The Old Guy's Lament," in *Poems for Men,* p. 186.

*Chapter Six*

1. Heywood Broun, "Introduction," *The Damon Runyon Omnibus*, p. 3.
2. Hoyt, p. 174.
3. Nunnally Johnson, "Runyon Money-Ball," *New Yorker* 20 (July 2, 1944): 6.
4. Damon Runyon, "Ransom . . . $1,000,000," in *More Guys and Dolls*, p. 3.
5. Anon., "Broadway Tales," *New York Times*, August 12, 1934, p. 7.
6. Fred T. Marsh, "The Best of Runyon," *New York Times*, March 13, 1938, p. 16.
7. Gene Fowler, *Skyline: A Reporter's Reminiscence of the 1920s* (New York, 1961), p. 72.
8. Anon., "Broadway Types," *New York Times*, September 6, 1931, p. 15.
9. Walter Winchell, "Foreword" to *Blue Plate Special*, in *The Damon Runyon Omnibus*, p. 344.
10. Walter Winchell, "Unforgetable Damon Runyon," *Readers Digest*, August 1968, p. 134.

*Chapter Seven*

1. Leon Surmelian, *Techniques of Fiction Writing* (Garden City, N.Y.: Doubleday and Co., 1968), p. 102.
2. Ed Weiner, *The Damon Runyon Story* (New York, 1948), p. 139.
3. Evan Esar, *The Humor of Humor* (New York: Horizon Press, 1952), p. 31.
4. Henri Bergson, *Laughter: An Essay on the Meaning of the Comic*, trans. by Cloudesley Brereton and Fred Rothwell (New York: Macmillan, 1937), p. 133.
5. Ibid., p. 134.
6. Max Eastman, *The Enjoyment of Laughter* (New York: Simon and Schuster, New York, 1938), p. 70.
7. Damon Runyon, "Johnny One Eye," in *More Guys and Dolls*, p. 297.
8. Bergson, p. 128.

9. Herman Melville, *Billy Budd and the Critics* (Belmont, Calif.: Wadsworth Publishing Co., 1961), p. 10.

10. Leslie Stephen, *Swift* (New York: Harper and Brothers Publishers, n.d.), p. 169.

11. Wagner, pp. 46–47.

12. Bergson, p. 145.

13. Ibid., p. 97.

14. Ibid., p. 200.

15. Ibid., p. 12.

16. Damon Runyon, "Butch Minds the Baby," in *The Damon Runyon Omnibus*, p. 44.

17. Damon Runyon, "Runyon Writes on Pigs," *New York American*, March 14, 1921, p. 18.

*Chapter Eight*

1. Damon Runyon, "Your Neighbor—The Gambler," *Cosmopolitan Magazine*, November 1921, p. 66.

2. Calvin S. Brown, "The Luck of Little Miss Marker," *Western Humanities Review* 11 (1957): 342–43.

3. John O. Rees, "The Last Local Colorist: Damon Runyon," *Kansas Magazine* n.v. (1968): 80.

4. A. H. Lewis, *The Sunset Trail* (New York: A. L. Burt Co., 1905), p. 113.

5. A. H. Lewis, *The Apaches of New York* (Chicago: M. A. Donohue and Co., 1912), pp. 33–34.

6. Fowler, p. 24.

7. Walter Winchell, "Unforgetable Damon Runyon," p. 133.

8. Wagner, pp. 123–24.

9. Riemer, p. 403.

10. Kempton, p. 145.

11. Damon Runyon, "The Lemon Drop Kid," in *The Damon Runyon Omnibus*, p. 453.

12. Damon Runyon, "Little Miss Marker," in *The Damon Runyon Omnibus*, p. 426.

13. Claude M. Simpson, *The Local Colorists: American Short Stories, 1857–1900* (New York: Harper & Brothers Publishers, 1960), p. 13.

14. Bergson, p. 129.

15. Ibid., p. 15.

16. Surmelian, p. 209.

17. Damon Runyon, "Butch Minds the Baby," in *The Damon Runyon Omnibus*, p. 46.

18. Damon Runyon, "Damon Runyon's The Brighter Side," *New York Mirror*, February 11, 1942, p. 30.

19. Wagner, p. 92.

20. La Rocque Du Bose, "Damon Runyon's Underworld Lingo," *Texas University Studies in English* 32 (1953):125

21. Surmelian, p. 207.

22. Murray Godwin, "Broadway in Two Tenses," *New Republic* 68 (October 14, 1931):240.

23. Stuart Berg Flexner, "Preface," *Dictionary of American Slang* (New York: Thomas Crowell Company, 1966), p. xiii.

24. Bergson, p. 112.

25. Eastman, p. 102.

26. Anon., "Elegantes to Attend Revue to Aid Charity," *New York American*, January 5, 1930, p. M-1.

27. Anon., "Damon Runyon, 62, Columnist, Is Dead," *New York Times*, December 11, 1946, p. 31.

28. Weiner, p. 217.

*Chapter Nine*

1. Damon Runyon, "The Brighter Side," *New York Mirror*, December 30, 1937, p. 10.

2. Sally Fulton, "A Letter From London," *Saturday Review of Literature* 17 (December 4, 1937):42.

3. Anon., "What Is Runyonese?" *London Times Literary Supplement*, October 29, 1938, p. 691.

4. J.F.L., "More Late Than Somewhat," *Spectator*, October 8, 1937, p. 589.

5. E. C. Bentley, "Furthermore," *Spectator*, October 15, 1937, p. 636.

6. Phillip Van Doren, "Popular Shorts," *Saturday Review of Literature* 27 (July 29, 1944):20.

7. Kempton, p. 133.

8. Surmelian, p. 210.

9. Ibid., p. 209.

10. H. E. Bates, *The Modern Short Story: A Critical Survey* (Boston: The Writer Inc., Publishers, 1972), p. 166.

11. Fletcher Pratt, "Runyon's Broadway," *Saturday Review of Literature* 19 (January 28, 1939):17.

12. Hoyt, p. 253.

13. Anon., "Take It Easy," *London Times Literary Supplement,* October 29, 1938, p. 691.

14. Meyer Berger, "Runyon's New York," *New York Times*, August 21, 1949, p. 4.

15. John Lardner, "The Secret Past of a Popular Author," *New Yorker*, 25 (August 27, 1949): 58.

16. Stanley Jasspon Kunitz and Howard Haycraft, "Damon Runyon," *Twentieth Century Authors* (New York, 1942), p. 1211.

17. Lardner, p. 58.

18. Pratt, p. 17.

19. Riemer, p. 405.

20. Anon., "Was Runyon Century's Best Sports Writer?" *Editor and Publisher* 83 (February 18, 1950):29.

21. David W. Maurer, "Gumming Up the Syntax," *Nation* 206 (October 31, 1966):456.

22. Hoyt, p. 250.

23. Rees, p. 79.

24. Kunitz and Haycraft, p. 1211.

25. Hoyt, p. 268.

# Selected Bibliography

## PRIMARY SOURCES

### 1. Short Stories
*The Best of Damon Runyon*. New York: Frederick A. Stokes, 1938.
*Blue Plate Special*. New York: Frederick A. Stokes, 1934.
*The Damon Runyon Omnibus*. Garden City, N.Y.: Sun Dial Press, 1944.
*Guys and Dolls*. New York: Frederick A. Stokes, 1931.
*Money From Home*. New York: Frederick A. Stokes, 1935.
*More Guys and Dolls*. Garden City, N.Y.: Garden City Books, 1951.
*Runyon a la Carte*. Philadelphia: J. B. Lippincott, 1944.
*Runyon First and Last*. Philadelphia: J. B. Lippincott, 1949.
*Take It Easy*. New York: Frederick A. Stokes, 1938.

### 2. Newspaper Columns
*In Our Town*. New York: Creative Age Press, 1946.
*My Old Man*. New York: Stackpole Sons, 1939.
*My Wife Ethel*. Philadelphia: David McKay, 1939.
*Short Takes: Readers' Choice of the Best Columns of America's Favorite Newspaperman*. New York: Somerset Books, 1946.
*Trials and Other Tribulations*. Philadelphia: J. B. Lippincott, 1948.
*The Turps*. London: Constable, 1951.

### 3. Poetry
*Poems for Men*. Garden City, N.Y.: Permabooks, 1951.
*Rhymes of the Firing Line*. New York: Desmond Fitzgerald, 1912.
*The Tents of Trouble, Ballads of the Wanderbund and Other Verse*. New York: Desmond Fitzgerald, 1911.

4. Play

With Howard Lindsay. *A Slight Case of Murder*. New York: Dramatists
   Play Service, 1940.

5. Short Stories: Uncollected

"The Big Mitten." *Hampton's Magazine* 26 (June, 1911).
"Boss of Balar." *Metropolitan Magazine* 24 (July 1907).
"The Breed and the Ball." *Munsey's Magazine* 45 (May 1911).
"The Breeze Kid's Big Tear-Off." *Hampton's Magazine* 27 (January
   1912).
"Delegates at Large." *Cosmopolitan Magazine* 92 (July 1932).
"Fear." *All-Story Magazine* 12 (November 1908).
"Hole in the Horn of Plenty." *Munsey's Magazine* 48 (December 1912).
"The King of Kavanaugh County." *People's Magazine* n.v. (April
   1907).
"The Lady Member." *Hampton's Magazine* 26 (February 1911).
"Nose of Nemesis." *Munsey's Magazine* 48 (November 1912).
"Spirit of the West." *Hampton's Magazine* 25 (August 1910).

6. Articles: Uncollected

"The Greatest Racehorse I Ever Saw." *Cosmopolitan Magazine* 109
   (September 1940).
"An Interview with William Randolph Hearst." n.p., n.d., pamphlet,
   New York Public Library.
"Maurice McLaughlin, World's Greatest Tennis Player." *Munsey's
   Magazine* 53 (November 1914).
"Mr. 'B' and His Stork Club." *Cosmopolitan Magazine* 122 (May
   1947).
"The Twilight of the Gangster." *Cosmopolitan Magazine* 92 (June
   1932).
"Woman Boss of Denver." *Harper's Weekly* 52 (December 1908).
"Your Neighbor—The Gambler." *Cosmopolitan Magazine* 71 (November
   1921).

SECONDARY SOURCES

1. Books

Clark, Tom. *The World of Damon Runyon*. New York: Harper and

Row, 1978. A biography that also emphasizes contemporaries and current events.

Hoyt, Edwin P. *A Gentleman of Broadway*. Boston: Little, Brown, 1964. A comprehensive biography and critical analysis.

Runyon, Damon, Jr. *Father's Footsteps*. New York: Random House, 1954. Recalls his childhood and Runyon's last days.

Wagner, Jean. *Runyonese: The Mind and Craft of Damon Runyon*. Paris: Stechert-Hafner, 1965. A critical analysis of the short fiction.

Weiner, Ed. *The Damon Runyon Story*. New York: Longmans, Green, 1948. A biography based on contemporary information.


2. Essays, Reviews, and Sections of Books

Bayard, Charles L. "Me and Mr. Finch in Denver." *Colorado Magazine* 52 (1975). The young reporter as part of a chalk-talk news team.

Bentley, E. C. "Furthermore." *Spectator* 159 (October 15, 1937). Responds to J.F.L., acknowledging prior British edition.

————. "Introduction." *The Best of Damon Runyon*. New York: Triangle Books, 1940. Comedy and slang give life to Runyon's fictional characters.

Berger, Meyer. "Runyon's New York." *New York Times*, August 21, 1949. Old hometown sketches pale beside Broadway fairy tales.

Broun, Heywood. "Introduction." *The Damon Runyon Omnibus*. New York: Blue Ribbon Books, 1939. The Broadway characters are based on real people.

Brown, Calvin S. "The Luck of Little Miss Marker." *Western Humanities Review* 11 (1957). Similarities with Bret Harte's "The Outcasts of Poker Flat."

Du Bose, La Rocque. "Damon Runyon's Underworld Lingo." *Texas University Studies in English* 32 (1953). Nonliterary words surveyed in fifty-one short stories.

Fowler, Gene. *Skyline: A Reporter's Reminiscences of the 1920s*. New York: Viking Press, 1961. Recalls early days as reporter in New York.

Fulton, Sally. "A Letter From London." *Saturday Review of Literature* 17 (December 4, 1937). Controversy among British readers over slang.

Godwin, Murray. "Broadway in Two Tenses." *New Republic* 68 (October 14, 1931). Slang not as distinctive as use of two tenses.

Gordon, Arthur. "Runyon's Last Round." *Saturday Evening Post* 229 (December 8, 1956). Battle lost to cancer.

Iddon, Don. "Memoir of the Author." In Damon Runyon, *Short Takes*. London: Constable, 1948. Reminiscences of Runyon's last days as a newspaperman and a brief biography.

J.F.L. "More Late Than Somewhat." *Spectator* 159 (October 8, 1937). Runyonese comparison with Homer.

Johnson, Nunnally. "Runyon Money-Ball." *New Yorker* 20 (July 1, 1944). The narrator takes Broadway to World War II.

Kinnaird, Clark. "Introduction." *More Guys and Dolls: Thirty-four of the Best Short Stories by Damon Runyon*. Garden City, N.Y.: Garden City Books, 1951. Runyon preferred the Turps but artfully delineated the Broadway characters.

Kunitz, S. J., and Haycraft, Stanley. "Damon Runyon." In *Twentieth Century Authors*. New York: H. W. Wilson, 1942. Biography and current popularity in England.

Lardner, John. "The Secret Past of a Popular Author." *New Yorker* 25 (August 27, 1949). Authentic style was replaced by fairy tales.

Maisel, Albert Q. "Damon Runyon's Last Story—by His Friends." *Collier's Magazine* 125 (April 22, 1950). Great popularity brought contributions to cancer fund.

Maurer, D. W. "Gumming up the Syntax." *Nation* 206 (October 31, 1966). Review of Wagner's book.

Mencken, Henry Louis. *The American Language*. New York: Alfred A. Knopf, 1937. Listed as a maker of American slang.

————. *The American Language: Supplement I*. New York: Alfred A. Knopf, 1948. Sensitivity to language in treatise on the word "skibby."

————. *The American Language: Supplement II*. New York: Alfred A. Knopf, 1948. Compared with Ring Lardner.

Parker, Dan. "Damon Runyon Dies: Top Hearst Writer." *Editor and Publisher* 79 (December 14, 1946). Primarily remembered as a reporter.

Pratt, Fletcher. "Runyon's Broadway." *Saturday Review of Literature* 19 (January 28, 1939). His fiction has fidelity to reality.

Rees, John O. "The Last Local Colorist, Damon Runyon." *Kansas Magazine*, n.v. (1968). Influences of Bret Harte and A. H. Lewis.

Riemer, Svend. "Damon Runyon—Philosopher of City Life." *Social Forces* 25 (May 1947). A new regional literature in urban society.

"Runyon, Damon." *Current Biography, 1942,* n.v. Primarily a newspaperman but also a writer and movie producer.

"Runyon: Sports Writer Chafes in His Former Chief's Mantle." *News-Week* 9 (January 16, 1937). Runyon tried to replace Brisbane's editorials.

"Runyon with the Half-Boob Air." *Time* 48 (June 24, 1946). Quotes review of *Short Takes* by Runyon.

Spiller, Robert E.; Thorp, Willard; Johnson, Thomas H.; and Canby, Henry Seidel, eds. *Literary History of the United States.* New York: The Macmillan Company, 1957. More genial tone than Lardner's Ringlish."

Van Doren, Phillip. "Review of Runyon A La Carte." *Saturday Review of Literature* 27 (July 29, 1944). Both Runyon and James T. Farrell are repeating themselves.

"What Is Runyonese?" *London Times Literary Supplement,* October 29, 1939. Vocabulary more a literary creation than underworld slang.

Winchell, Walter. "Foreword." *The Damon Runyon Omnibus.* New York: Blue Ribbon Books, 1939. A great sports historian who also generates laughter in short stories and movies.

————. "Prelude to '30.'" In Ed Weiner, *The Damon Runyon Story.* New York: Longmans, Green, 1948. A farewell tribute from Runyon's perspective as a newspaper reporter.

————. "Unforgettable Damon Runyon." *Reader's Digest* 93 (August 1968). Nostalgic biography.

# Index

165